Getting to the Roots

of Social Studies Vocabulary

citizen independence democracy

Authors

Timothy Rasinski, Ph.D.

Nancy Padak, Ed.D.

Rick M. Newton, Ph.D.

Evangeline Newton, Ph.D.

SHELL EDUCATION

Publishing Credits

Robin Erickson, *Production Director*; Lee Aucoin, *Creative Director*;
Timothy J. Bradley, *Illustration Manager*; Sara Johnson, M.S.Ed., *Editorial Director*;
Jennifer Viñas, *Editor*; Grace Alba, *Designer*; Corinne Burton, M.A.Ed., *Publisher*

Image Credits

All images Shutterstock

Standards

© 2004 Mid-continent Research for Education and Learning (McREL)
© 2010 National Governors Association Center for Best Practices and Council of Chief State School Officers (CCSS)

Shell Education

5301 Oceanus Drive
Huntington Beach, CA 92649-1030
http://www.shelleducation.com
ISBN 978-1-4258-0868-6
© 2014 Shell Educational Publishing, Inc.

Table of Contents

Management

Lessons

Unit I—Rulers and Governments

Table of Contents

Social Studies Vocabulary Research and Practice

Words are labels for key concepts in social studies. Although learning these words is critical to student success, teaching them can be challenging. Asking students to look words up in their dictionaries or glossaries and then to memorize definitions provides, at best, a short-term solution. Many of the concepts are new to students, and most of the concepts are abstract. Moreover, students may have insufficient background knowledge to learn these new concepts well.

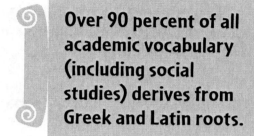

Over 90 percent of all academic vocabulary (including social studies) derives from Greek and Latin roots.

In this book, we present a systematic and research-based alternative to vocabulary learning: a roots approach. Because most words are defined (and spelled) by what their parts mean, students can expand their vocabularies by learning how to build words from the roots up. Over 90 percent of all academic vocabulary derives from Latin or Greek roots (prefixes, suffixes, bases).

The lessons in this book center on bases, which provide the core meaning in words. Prefixes, attached to the beginnings of words, and suffixes, attached to the endings of words, are used throughout the book, but the focus is on 25 Latin and Greek roots that generate hundreds of social studies words. As students learn these word parts and recognize them as the essential components in specific words from social studies, their growing verbal skills support their increasing ability to comprehend social studies principles as well as to increase and enhance their general vocabulary.

What Does Research Say About Using a Roots Approach?

The size and depth of students' vocabulary is associated with proficiency in reading comprehension. (Baumann et al. 2002; Beck, Perfetti, and McKeown 1982; Kame'enui, Carnine, and Freschi 1982; Stahl and Fairbanks 1986).

Morphological analysis (e.g., via a roots approach) is important because it is generative and allows students to make connections among semantically related words or word families (Nagy and Scott 2000). In fact, developing morphological awareness is an integral component of word learning (Biemiller and Slonim 2001). In a comprehensive review of 16 studies analyzing the effect of instruction in morphological awareness on literacy achievement, Carlisle (2010) observes that "People learn morphemes as they learn language" (465).

Social Studies Vocabulary Research and Practice *(cont.)*

Classroom-based studies have demonstrated the effectiveness of teaching word parts and context clues in the primary and intermediate grades (Baumann et al. 2002; Baumann et al. 2005; Biemiller 2005; Carlisle 2000; Kieffer and Lesaux 2007; Mountain 2005; Porter-Collier 2010). Research in content-area vocabulary has demonstrated the effectiveness of teaching Greek and Latin word roots, especially for struggling readers (Harmon, Hedrick, and Wood 2005). Moreover, vocabulary knowledge is associated with higher scores on high-stakes tests like the ACT; students with knowledge of Latin score significantly higher on the SAT than those without such knowledge (ACT 2006; LaFleur 1981).

No single instructional method is sufficient. Teachers need a variety of methods that teach word meanings while also increasing the depth of word knowledge (Blachowicz et al. 2006; Lehr, Osborn, and Hiebert 2004). These methods should aim at fostering:

Immersion

Students need frequent opportunities to use new words in diverse oral and print contexts in order to learn them thoroughly (Blachowicz and Fisher 2006).

Metacognitive and metalinguistic awareness

Students must understand and know how to manipulate the structural features of language (Nagy and Scott 2000).

Word consciousness

Word exploration (e.g., etymology) and word play (e.g., puns, riddles, games) help students develop an awareness of and interest in words (Graves and Watts-Taffe 2002; Lehr, Osborn, and Hiebert 2004).

Social Studies Vocabulary Research and Practice (cont.)

Why Teach with a Roots Approach?

Teaching with a roots approach is efficient. Over 60 percent of the words students encounter in their reading have recognizable word parts (Nagy et al. 1989). Moreover, content-area vocabulary is largely of Greek and Latin origin (Harmon, Hedrick, and Wood 2005). Many words from Greek and Latin roots meet the criteria for "tier two" words and are appropriate for instruction (Beck, McKeown, and Kucan 2002).

Root study promotes independent word learning (Carlisle 2010). In addition, students learn to make connections among words that are semantically related (Nagy and Scott 2000). Research suggests that the brain is a pattern detector (Cunningham 2004). Latin and Greek word roots follow linguistic patterns that can help students with the meaning, sound, and spelling of English words. Indeed, Latin and Greek roots have consistent orthographic (spelling) patterns (Rasinski and Padak 2013; Bear et al. 2011).

Many English language learners speak first languages semantically related to Latin. For example, more than 75 percent of the words in Spanish come from Latin (Chandler and Schwartz 1961, 1991). In fact, Spanish, Portuguese, French, Catalan, Italian, and Rumanian are all classified as "Romance Languages" because they derive from Latin, the language of ancient Romans. Enhancing this natural linguistic connection inherent in many of these languages can accelerate these students' vocabulary growth (Blachowicz et al. 2006).

Many states are beginning to include root study in their elementary and middle school literacy standards. Indeed, the *Common Core State Standards* focus extensively on root-specific standards in the "Reading Foundational Skills" and "Language/Vocabulary Acquisition and Use" sections. According to these standards, attention to roots should begin in kindergarten.

prefix

A root at the beginning of a word. For example, in the word *segregate*, the initial *se-* is a prefix, meaning "aside," "apart."

base

The core root, which provides a word with its basic meaning. In the word *segregate*, the base is *greg-*, which means "flock," herd."

suffix

A root that ends a word. In the word *segregate*, the final *-ate* is a verbal suffix, meaning "to do."

Note: You can find out more about what prefixes and suffixes do on the Digital Resource CD (filename: functions.pdf).

What Is a Root?

A *root* is a word part that contains meaning (and not merely sound). Roots are vocabulary multipliers—each root taught helps students discover the meaning to multiple words. The three types of roots, depending on their placement within a word, are prefix, base, and suffix.

Social Studies Vocabulary Research and Practice (cont.)

Differentiating Instruction

Some students may need additional support. Others may benefit from additional challenge. These ideas may help you differentiate instruction:

- Use visual aids.

- Ask students to sketch or act out words. Others can guess the depicted words.

- Reduce length of activity.

- Pair students. Encourage them to talk about the roots and the activities.

- Challenge students to create new words that contain the root.

- Talk students through the necessary process to complete an activity. Your aim should be to scaffold students' thinking, not to provide answers.

- Alert other teachers (mathematics, science, etc.) of the roots you are working on with students. Ask them to include them, when possible, in their own instruction with students.

- Have students keep a personal vocabulary journal in which they list the roots and related words they learn. Encourage students to use their new vocabulary in their oral and written language (e.g., "Use at least one word containing the [demo-] root in your social studies journal entry today.")

- Put the roots and words derived from the roots on display in the classroom. Keep them on display over the course of several weeks. (You may wish to move some of the displays into the hallway or other sites outside your classroom.)

- Play word games that involve the roots with your students often. Word lists containing the roots in this book are found on the Digital Resource CD (filename: wordlists.pdf).

Students who need additional challenge can a) look for words containing the featured root in their content-area texts, b) write riddles for others to solve, using several words that contain the root, or c) use an online resource to find additional words containing the root (e.g., http://www.onelook.com) or to create word puzzles featuring the root (e.g., http://www.puzzlemaker.com).

Like their peers, English language learners benefit from the focus on meaning using research-based strategies to learn new roots and words. Especially if students' native languages derive from Latin (e.g., Spanish), make comparisons to the native languages whenever possible. (You can look online for resources to assist with this.) When Spanish speakers learn to look for roots within words, they will be able to relate many word roots in English to their counterparts in Spanish. Sharing their knowledge with other classmates will help everyone grow.

How to Use This Book

The following information will help you implement each lesson.

Lesson Overview

A list of **Standards** (McREL and Common Core State Standards) is included in each lesson.

The **Materials** listed include the activity pages for students.

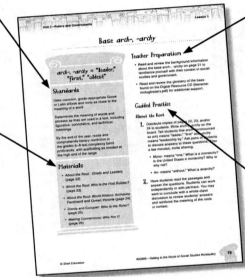

Each lesson begins with a **Teacher Preparation** that provides essential information about the root. Reading this section before you teach the lesson will provide you with a foundation to ensure student success.

The **Guided Practice** portion of each lesson includes suggestions for implementing each of the student activity pages.

Before beginning each lesson, review the **Teacher Background Information and Tips** page to provide additional help for students. Additional information to introduce each unit can be found on pages 12–13.

The **About the Root** activities are introductions and include short passages using the root of focus. The purpose of these passages is to show students contextual use of the root in social studies. As students read to themselves or listen to the teacher read aloud, they identify words containing the roots in extended texts that center on a wide range of interesting topics.

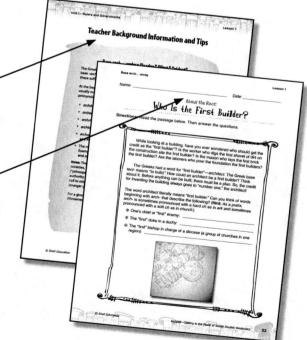

How to Use This Book (cont.)

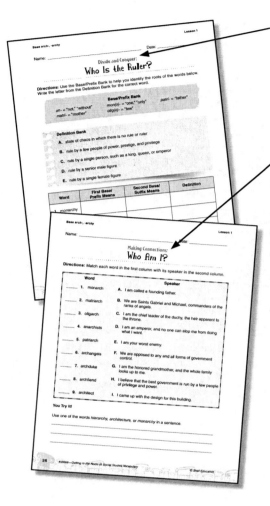

The **Divide and Conquer** activities allow students to pull words apart. They dissect the parts of the words, understand the meaning of these parts, and then gain a greater understanding of the word as a whole.

The **Making Connections** activities allow students to use their knowledge of roots to make connections to vocabulary and offer students the opportunity to extend their exploration of the root(s) through activities such as word sorts, riddles, representing the roots and related words in drawings, and game-like tasks. They may need to distinguish when to use a certain root or which way the root is used in a word.

All of the student activity pages and additional resources such as word lists and flashcards can be found on the **Digital Resource CD**.

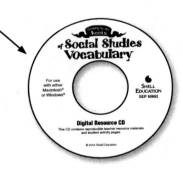

How to Use This Book (cont.)

Tips for Implementation

These tips will help you think about how to teach the lessons in this book.

* You will find many suggestions in this text, but remember that they are just that— suggestions. You should feel free to adapt the lessons to meet your students' needs.

* Plan to spend five to ten minutes per day on vocabulary related to social studies.

* You can teach the lessons in any order. You may want to coordinate with your curriculum. Each lesson addresses one basic social studies idea or concept. You can also expand on any lesson as you see fit. If students need more work on a particular root, you may wish to use some of the additional practice activities described in Appendix C.

* Before beginning a new lesson, read the Teacher Background Information and Tips page. These notes provide general information and identify many social studies words built on the base of the lesson.

* Talking about the roots is very important for student learning. This approach to vocabulary development goes far beyond mere memorization of specific words (which, according to research, does not work). Students need to learn to think about how roots contribute to meanings. Talking this through can help them develop this realization. So, encourage students to talk, Talk, TALK!!!

* Each week, display the root(s) and meaning(s) prominently in your classroom.

* Encourage students to use the root as much as possible throughout the entire week. Reading, writing, speaking, and listening to words containing the root will facilitate learning. Several generic activities (see Appendix C) provide additional instruction or practice, if you or your students wish.

* You may wish to provide students with dictionaries as they work through the activities sheets.

How to Use This Book *(cont.)*

Introducing Each Unit

Refer to the following information before beginning each unit:

Unit I–Rulers and Government

Social studies involves the study of governments and leaders. Many of the essential concepts and vocabulary related to governments and leaders are derived from Greek and Latin roots. In Unit I, students have the opportunity to explore five of these roots—what they mean and how they have been used to create the vocabulary of leaders and governments. By studying these roots, students will better understand why Abraham Lincoln described American *democracy* as "government of the people, by the people, and for the people." Roots addressed in this unit are:

- Greek Base *arch-, -archy* = "leader," "first," "oldest"
- Greek Base *-crat, -cracy* = "rule," "ruler"
- Latin Base *dic-, dict-* = "say," "speak," "tell"
- Latin Base *judg-, judic-* = "judge," "decide"
- Latin Base *popul-* and Greek Base *dem(o)-* = "the people"

Unit II–Cities and Civics

Governments represent groups of people or communities. In Unit II, students will learn about word roots that the Greeks and Romans used to help them organize and maintain their cities and other communities. These roots are still used today in the words that we use to organize our communities and engage in civic activities. As students follow the *sequence* of lessons in this unit, they are certain to *integrate* these roots into their own vocabularies. Roots addressed in this unit are:

- Latin base *urb-, urban-* and Greek base *poli-, -polis* = "city"
- Latin bases *civ-, cit-, civil-* = "citizen" and *milit-* = "soldier," "fighter"
- Latin Base *sequ-, secut-* = "follow"
- Latin bases *equ(i)-, egal-* = "equal," "fair"
- Latin bases *greg-* = "flock," "herd" and *integr-* = "whole"

How to Use This Book (cont.)

Introducing Each Unit (cont.)

Unit III—Cultures and Beliefs

Religion and religious beliefs often play an important role in many cultures and societies. This was certainly true of Greek and Roman societies. Thus, many word roots referring to God and religion are drawn from Greek and Latin. In Unit III, students will learn about word roots that the Greeks and Romans used to help them shape and share their religious beliefs. Many of the words we use today in English that refer to a supreme being, human beings, how we think, what we believe in, and how we change in our thinking and beliefs originate in the Greek and Latin roots students will study in this unit. We think this is an *incredible* unit. We hope you think so, too. Roots addressed in this unit are:

* Greek base *the(o)-* and Latin base *de(i)-, divin-* = "god"

* Latin base *vert-, vers-* = "turn," "change"

* Latin base *human-* and Greek base *anthrop(o)-* = "mankind," "human being"

* Latin bases *serv-, servat-* = "keep," "save" and *liber-, liberat-* = "free"

* Latin bases *fid-, fidel-* = "faith," "trust" and *cred-, credit-* = "believe"

Unit IV—History

As in current times, ancient civilizations experienced times of war and times of peace, times for building and times for destruction. In Unit IV, students will discover that the Greeks and Romans had key word roots to express and expand on these ideas. Many of the words that we use today for communicating about war and peace, building and destroying, moving forward and sometimes moving backward in our ideas and over time come from the Greeks and Romans. We hope students are discovering that as they *progress* in their knowledge of Greek and Latin word roots, they are building for themselves an *indestructible* vocabulary. Roots addressed in this unit are:

* Latin bases *bell-* = "war" and *pac-* = "peace"

* Latin base *annu-, enni-* = "year"

* Latin base *stru-, struct-* = "build"

* Latin bases *grad-, gress-* = "step," "go"

* Latin base *cid-, cis-* = "cut," "kill"

How to Use This Book (cont.)

Introducing Each Lesson

Introduce each root by linking to words students already know. You could:

- Put two or three common words containing the root on the board and ask students to talk about what meaning they share. You may want to embed these words in phrases or include quick sketches, if applicable. By perusing the Teacher Notes, you will readily find a large number of derivatives. You may also wish to print word lists found on the Digital Resource CD (filename: wordlists.pdf) for students. Select words which you think your students will recognize.

- Tell students, "The root of the week is _____. It means _____." Ask them to work with partners to generate words containing the root. Make a class list, and discuss common meaning.

- Encourage students to use the root's definition in their talk about words containing the root.

Assessment

At least one part of each lesson could be used for assessment purposes. Suggestions for assessment include:

- Use a knowledge rating chart with students. To do this, select key words from something students will read. Make a three-column chart for students to indicate if they a) know a word well, b) have seen or heard it, or c) don't know it at all.

- Have students keep word journals in which they a) record information about roots and the words that contain them or b) keep lists of interesting words from their reading. Ask students to peruse their journals occasionally to draw some conclusions about their word knowledge.

- Encourage students to use self-assessment. Ask them to write about a) their own word knowledge, b) where they find new and interesting words, and/or c) what strategies they use most often to figure out the meaning of new words.

Correlation to the Standards

Shell Education is committed to producing educational materials that are research and standards based. In this effort, we have correlated all of our products to the academic standards of all 50 United States, the District of Columbia, the Department of Defense Dependent Schools, and all Canadian provinces.

How To Find Standards Correlations

To print a customized correlation report of this product for your state, visit our website at http://www.shelleducation.com and follow the on-screen directions. If you require assistance in printing correlation reports, please contact Customer Service at 1-877-777-3450.

Purpose and Intent of Standards

Legislation mandates that all states adopt academic standards that identify the skills students will learn in kindergarten through grade twelve. Many states also have standards for Pre–K. This same legislation sets requirements to ensure the standards are detailed and comprehensive.

Standards are designed to focus instruction and guide adoption of curricula. Standards are statements that describe the criteria necessary for students to meet specific academic goals. They define the knowledge, skills, and content students should acquire at each level. Standards are also used to develop standardized tests to evaluate students' academic progress. Teachers are required to demonstrate how their lessons meet state standards. State standards are used in the development of all of our products, so educators can be assured they meet the academic requirements of each state.

Common Core State Standards

Many lessons in this book are aligned to the Common Core State Standards (CCSS). The standards support the objectives presented throughout the lessons and are provided on the Digital Resource CD (filename: standards.pdf).

McREL Compendium

We use the Mid-continent Research for Education and Learning (McREL) Compendium to create standards correlations. Each year, McREL analyzes state standards and revises the compendium. By following this procedure, McREL is able to produce a general compilation of national standards. Each lesson in this product is based on one or more McREL standards, which are provided on the Digital Resource CD (filename: standards.pdf).

TESOL and WIDA Standards

The lessons in this book promote English language development for English language learners. The standards listed on the Digital Resource CD (filename: standards.pdf) support the language objectives presented throughout the lessons.

Standards Chart

McREL Standards	Lessons
Language Arts 5.1—Establishes and adjusts purposes for reading	All Lessons
Language Arts 5.4—Uses word origins and derivations to understand word meaning	All Lessons
Common Core State Standards	**Lessons**
Literacy L.6-8.4b—Use common, grade-appropriate Greek or Latin affixes and roots as clues to the meaning of a word	All Lessons
Literacy.RH.6-8.4—Determine the meaning of words and phrases as they are used in a text, including vocabulary specific to domains related to history/social studies	All Lessons
Literacy RI.6-8.4—Determine the meaning of words and phrases as they are used in a text, including figurative, connotative, and technical meanings	All Lessons
Literacy RI.6-8.10—By the end of the year, read and comprehend literary nonfiction in the grades 6–8 text complexity band proficiently, with scaffolding as needed at the high end of the range	All Lessons
TESOL and WIDA Standards	**Lessons**
English language learners **communicate** for **social**, **intercultural**, and **instructional** purposes within the school setting.	All Lessons
English language learners **communicate** information, ideas, and concepts necessary for academic success in the area of **language arts**.	All Lessons

Concept Correlations

The following lessons are especially useful during the instruction of the concepts listed below.

Concept	Lessons
Rulers and Governments	Unit I: Lesson 1–Lesson 5 (pages 19–58)
Cities and Civics	Unit II: Lesson 1–Lesson 5 (pages 59–97)
Cultures and Beliefs	Unit III: Lesson 1–Lesson 5 (pages 98–137)
History	Unit IV: Lesson 1–Lesson 5 (pages 138–177)

About the Authors

Timothy Rasinski, Ph.D., is a professor of literacy education at Kent State University. He has written over 150 articles and has authored, coauthored, or edited over 15 books and curriculum programs on reading education. His research on reading has been cited by the National Reading Panel and has been published in journals such as *Reading Research Quarterly, The Reading Teacher, Reading Psychology*, and *The Journal of Educational Research*. Tim served on the Board of Directors of the International Reading Association, and from 1992–1999, he was coeditor of *The Reading Teacher*, the world's most widely read journal of literacy education. He has also served as editor of the *Journal of Literacy Research*, one of the premier research journals in reading. Tim is a past president of the College Reading Association, and he has won the A.B. Herr Award from the College Reading Association for his scholarly contributions to literacy education. In 2010, Tim was elected into the International Reading Hall of Fame.

Nancy Padak, Ed.D., is an active researcher, author, and consultant. She was a Distinguished Professor in the College and Graduate School of Education, Health, and Human Services at Kent State University. She directed KSU's Reading and Writing Center and taught in the area of literacy education. She was the Principal Investigator for the Ohio Literacy Resource Center, which has provided support for adult and family literacy programs since 1993. Prior to her arrival at Kent State in 1985, she was a classroom teacher and district administrator. She has written or edited more than 25 books and more than 90 chapters and articles. She has also served in a variety of leadership roles in professional organizations, including the presidency of the College Reading Association and (with others) the Editor of *The Reading Teacher* and the *Journal of Literacy Research*. She has won several awards for her scholarship and contributions to literacy education.

About the Authors (cont.)

Rick M. Newton, Ph.D., holds a doctoral degree in Greek and Latin from the University of Michigan and is now an emeritus professor of Greek and Latin at Kent State University. He developed the course "English Words from Classical Elements," which more than 15,000 Kent State students have taken over the past 30 years. He holds the Distinguished Teaching Award from the Kent State College of Arts and Sciences and the Translation Award from the Modern Greek Studies Association of North America and Canada.

Evangeline Newton, Ph.D., is a professor of literacy education at the University of Akron, where she served as the first director of the Center for Literacy. She teaches a variety of literacy methods courses and professional development workshops to elementary, middle, and high school teachers. A former coeditor of *The Ohio Reading Teacher*, Evangeline currently chairs the Reading Review Board of the Ohio Resource Center for Mathematics, Science, and Reading. She serves on editorial review boards for *The Reading Teacher* and *Reading Horizons*. Evangeline is active in the Association of Literacy Educators and the International Reading Association (IRA). As a participant in IRA's Reading and Writing for Critical Thinking project, Evangeline taught workshops for teachers and Peace Corps volunteers in Armenia. A former St. Louis public school teacher, Evangeline holds a B.A. from Washington University in St. Louis, an M.A.T. from Webster University, and a Ph.D. from Kent State University.

Base arch-, -archy

arch-, -archy = "leader," "first," "oldest"

Standards

Uses common, grade-appropriate Greek or Latin affixes and roots as clues to the meaning of a word

Determines the meaning of words and phrases as they are used in a text, including figurative, connotative, and technical meanings

By the end of the year, reads and comprehends literary nonfiction in the grades 6–8 text complexity band proficiently, with scaffolding as needed at the high end of the range

Materials

- About the Root: Chiefs and Leaders (page 22)

- About the Root: Who Is the First Builder? (page 23)

- About the Root: World History: Archduke Ferdinand and Queen Victoria (page 24)

- Divide and Conquer: Who Is the Ruler? (page 25)

- Making Connections: Who Am I? (page 26)

Teacher Preparation

- Read and review the background information about the base arch-, -archy on page 21 to familiarize yourself with their context in social studies and government.

- Read and review the glossary of the base found on the Digital Resource CD (filename: rootsglossary.pdf) for additional support.

Guided Practice

About the Root

1. Distribute copies of pages 22, 23, and/or 24 to students. Write arch-, -archy on the board. Tell students that arch- (pronounced as ark) means "leader," "first" and -archy means "leadership by." Ask pairs of students to discuss answers to these questions. After a few minutes, invite sharing.

    - Mono- means "one." What is a monarchy? Is the United States a monarchy? Why or why not?

    - An- means "without." What is anarchy?

2. Have students read the passages and answer the questions. Students can work independently or with partners. You may want to conclude with a whole-class discussion to review students' answers and reinforce the meaning of the roots in context.

Base arch-, -archy (cont.)

Divide and Conquer

3. Distribute copies of *Divide and Conquer* (page 25). As you guide students through the activity page, use questions like these to generate discussion about each of the words:

- Where is the meaning of "leader," "first" or "leadership by" in the word _____?

- Where might you see the word _____?

- Can you think of an example of _____?

Making Connections

4. Distribute copies of *Making Connections* (page 26).

5. Have students read all of the definitions before completing the activity sheet.

6. Conclude with a whole-class discussion that focuses on root meaning.

Words with arch-, -archy

anarchist
anarchy
archaeologist
archaeology
archaic
archaism
archangel
archbishop
archduke
archenemy
archeologist
archeology
architect
architecture
archives
archrival
hierarch
hierarchical
hierarchy
matriarch
matriarchal
matriarchy
monarch
oligarch
oligarchy
patriarch

A list of words to print out for students can be found on the Digital Resource CD (filename: wordlists.pdf).

Teacher Background Information and Tips

Base *arch-*, *-archy* = "leader," "first," "oldest"

The Greek base *arch-* (pronounced as "ark") means "leader," "first," and the Greek base *-archy* means "leadership by …." Important social studies words ending in these suffixes are *patriarch, matriarch, monarch, oligarch, anarchy,* and *hierarchy.*

At the beginning of a word, the root *arch-* (usually pronounced as "arch") usually means "first" or "oldest." Example words from social studies with this pronunciation include:

* *archduke:* the "first" duke or leader of a duchy

* *archenemy:* one's prime, chief, or "first" foe

* *archrival:* one's prime, or "first," opponent

* *archbishop:* the "first" bishop in a diocese who oversees other bishops

* *archangel:* the "first" angel in power among other angels. In the Bible, Gabriel and Michael are *Archangels*

* The root *arch-* also functions as a base, meaning "oldest" or "ancient." Example words from social studies include: *archives, archeologists, archaic,* and *archaism.*

Note: The meanings "leader," "first," "oldest" are related. In traditional patriarchal societies, for example, the firstborn son would inherit the throne from his father ("primogeniture"). Hence, the eldest son was considered to have the greatest authority and became the leader or ruler. The words *patriarch* and *matriarch* call to mind elderly father and mother figures who command respect from younger generations.

For a glossary of words with this root, see the Digital Resource CD (filename: rootsglossary.pdf).

Name: _____ Date: _____

About the Root:
Chiefs and Leaders

Directions: Read the information below. Then answer the questions.

The Greek bases *-arch* and *-archy* (pronounced as *ark* and *AHR-kee*) appear in many words describing "leaders" and those who are "first" in power. Answer these questions:

◎ The Greek base *mon(o)* means "one" or "only." How many people lead a *monarchy*? How do you know?

_____

_____

_____

◎ The Latin base *patr(i)* means "father." The ancient Hebrews had a *patriarchal* society. What can you tell about their leaders?

_____

_____

_____

At the beginning of words, *arch-* (pronounced with a soft *ch*, as in *church*) often means the "first" or chief figure.

Work with a partner to answer these questions. Use the meaning of *arch-* in your answers.

◎ Who is your favorite sports team's *archrival*? Why?

_____

_____

_____

◎ Who were the *archenemies* of the United States during World War II?

_____

_____

Name: _____ Date: _____

About the Root:
Who Is the First Builder?

Directions: Read the passage below. Then answer the questions.

While looking at a building, have you ever wondered who should get the credit as the "first builder"? Is the worker who digs the first shovel of dirt on the construction site the first builder? Is the mason who lays the first brick the first builder? Are the laborers who pour the foundation the first builders?

The Greeks had a word for "first builder"—*architect*. The Greek base *tect-* means "to build." How could an architect be a first builder? Think about it. Before anything can be built, there must be a plan. So, the credit for inventing the building always goes to "number one," the architect!

The word *architect* literally means "first builder." Can you think of words beginning with *arch-* that describe the following? (**Hint:** As a prefix, *arch-* is sometimes pronounced with a hard *ch* as in *ark* and sometimes pronounced with a soft *ch* as in *church*.)

◎ One's chief or "first" enemy: _____

◎ The "first" duke in a duchy: _____

◎ The "first" bishop in charge of a diocese (a group of churches in one region): _____

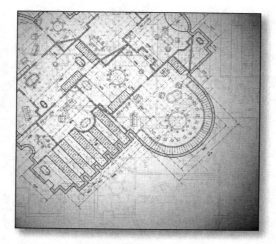

Name: _____   Date: _____

About the Root: World History:

Archduke Ferdinand and Queen Victoria

Directions: Read the passages. Then answer the questions on a separate sheet of paper.

A murder started World War I (1914–1918). On June 28, 1914, a member of a Serbian secret military society shot *Archduke* Franz Ferdinand of Austria-Hungary. As Archduke, Ferdinand was the "first" of all the dukes in the region. He was next in line to become king. His murder affected several different countries. In fact, 32 nations eventually fought in World War I.

◎ How are the terms *archduke* and *architect* similar? How do they mean "leader," "first," or "oldest"?

◎ List three ways in which *archduke* and *architect* are different from each other.

Queen Victoria was the *monarch* of the United Kingdom (UK) from 1837–1901. She ruled for more than 63 years. This is the longest reign of any female in history. By the time she became queen, the UK had a constitutional *monarchy*, so she had little direct power. Instead, she worked privately to influence activity. While she was doing this, she had nine children. They and 26 of her 34 grandchildren all married into European royal families. Victoria was a *matriarch*. She was called the "grandmother of Europe."

◎ Queen Victoria was both a *matriarch* and a *monarch*. How are the meanings of these two words similar? How are they different?

◎ Upon Queen Victoria's death, her son Edward became king. Was King Edward a *monarch* or a *matriarch*? Why?

Name: _____ Date: _____

Divide and Conquer:
Who Is the Ruler?

Directions: Use the Base/Prefix Bank to help you identify the roots of the words below. Write the letter from the Definition Bank for the correct word.

Base/Prefix Bank

an- = "not," "without"   *mon(o)-* = "one," "only"   *patri-* = "father"

matri- = "mother"   *olig(o)-* = "few"

Definition Bank

A. state of chaos in which there is no rule or ruler

B. rule by a few people of power, prestige, and privilege

C. rule by a single person, such as a king, queen, or emperor

D. rule by a senior male figure

E. rule by a single female figure

Word	First Base/ Prefix Means	Second Base/ Suffix Means	Definition
1. monarchy			
2. oligarchy			
3. matriarchy			
4. patriarchy			
5. anarchy			

Name: _____ Date: _____

Making Connections:
Who Am I?

. . . .

Directions: Match each word in the first column with its speaker in the second column.

Word	Speaker
_____ 1. monarch	**A.** I am called a founding father.
_____ 2. matriarch	**B.** We are Saints Gabriel and Michael, commanders of the ranks of angels.
_____ 3. oligarch	**C.** I am the chief leader of the duchy, the heir apparent to the throne.
_____ 4. anarchists	**D.** I am an emperor, and no one can stop me from doing what I want.
_____ 5. patriarch	**E.** I am your worst enemy.
_____ 6. archangels	**F.** We are opposed to any and all forms of government control.
_____ 7. archduke	**G.** I am the honored grandmother, and the whole family looks up to me.
_____ 8. archfiend	**H.** I believe that the best government is run by a few people of privilege and power.
_____ 9. architect	**I.** I came up with the design for this building.

You Try It!

Use one of the words *hierarchy, architecture,* or *monarchy* in a sentence.

_____

_____

_____

Base -crat, -cracy

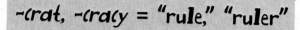

-crat, -cracy = "rule," "ruler"

Standards

Uses common, grade-appropriate Greek or Latin affixes and roots as clues to the meaning of a word

Determines the meaning of words and phrases as they are used in a text, including vocabulary specific to domains related to history/social studies

By the end of the year, reads and comprehends literary nonfiction in the grades 6–8 text complexity band proficiently, with scaffolding as needed at the high end of the range

Materials

- *About the Root: Ancient History: What Is an Aristocracy?* (page 30)

- *About the Root: Government: What Is an Autocracy?* (page 31)

- *About the Root: Government: What Is a Bureaucracy?* (page 32)

- *Divide and Conquer: Who Is the Ruler?* (page 33)

- *Making Connections: Who/What Am I?* (page 34)

Teacher Preparation

- Read and review the background information about the base *-crat, -cracy* on page 29 to familiarize yourself with their context in social studies and government.

- Read and review the glossary of the base found on the Digital Resource CD (filename: rootsglossary.pdf) for additional support.

Guided Practice

About the Root

1. Distribute copies of pages 30, 31, and/or 32 to students. Ask pairs of students to discuss answers to the questions below. After a few minutes, invite sharing.

   - *Auto-* means "self." What is an *autocracy*?

   - Could a *monarch* be an *autocrat*? Why or why not?

2. Have students read the passages and answer the questions. Students can work independently or with partners. You may want to conclude with a whole-class discussion to review students' answers and reinforce the meaning of the roots in context.

Base -crat, -cracy *(cont.)*

Divide and Conquer

3. Distribute copies of *Divide and Conquer* (page 33). As you guide students through the activity page, use questions like these to generate discussion about each of the words:

- Where is the meaning of "rule," "ruler," or "one who believes in rule by" in the word _____?

- Where might you see the word _____?

- Can you think of an example of _____?

Making Connections

4. Distribute copies of *Making Connections* (page 34).

5. Have students read all of the definitions before completing the activity sheet. To conclude, you can invite whole-class discussion. Focus on root meaning within the words and ask students which was easiest or most challenging to figure out. You could also ask pairs of students to change the form of words—from a word for a person (e.g., *bureaucrat*) to a word for a form of government or organization (e.g., *bureaucracy*) to a word describing either (e.g., *bureaucratic*).

Words with -crat, -cracy

aristocracy

aristocrat

aristocratic

autocracy

autocrat

autocratic

bureaucracy

bureaucrat

bureaucratic

democracy

democrat

democratic

gerontocracy

gynecocracy

gynocracy

plutocracy

plutocrat

plutocratic

theocracy

theocrat

theocratic

A list of words to print out for students can be found on the Digital Resource CD (filename: wordlists.pdf).

Spelling Hints:

Beginning with the consonant *c*, -crat and -cracy frequently attach to other roots by a connecting *o*. Additional endings may attach to the suffix -crat to form such adjectives as *democratic, aristocratic, plutocratic, theocratic, autocratic,* and *bureaucratic*.

Teacher Background Information and Tips

Base -*crat*, -*cracy* = "rule," "ruler"

The Greek base -*crat* means "ruler," "one who believes in rule by." The base -*cracy* means "rule by …." When describing governmental systems, -*crat* and -*cracy* are identical in meaning to -*arch* and -*archy* (presented in the previous lesson).

Additional endings may attach to the suffix -*crat* to form such adjectives as *democratic, aristocratic, plutocratic, theocratic, autocratic, bureaucratic*.

Important social studies words with these bases include *democracy, aristocracy, plutocracy, theocracy, autocracy, gynecocracy, gerontocracy,* and *bureaucracy*.

For a glossary of words with this root, see the Digital Resource CD (filename: rootsglossary.pdf).

Name: _____ Date: _____

About the Root: Ancient History:
What Is an Aristocracy?

Directions: Read the information below. Then answer the questions.

> The Greek bases -*crat* and -*cracy* appear in many words describing "rulers" (-*crat*) and those who "believe in rule by" certain people (-*cracy*). Because these bases begin with the consonant *c*, they are usually preceded by a connecting *o*. To determine who the ruler is in a word ending in -*crat* or -*cracy*, we "divide and conquer" at the connecting *o* and look to see what the word parts mean.

Work with a partner to answer these questions:

◎ The Greek base *dem(o)-* means "the people." How are leaders in a *democratic* society selected?

_____

_____

_____

◎ Is your school a *democracy*? Why or why not?

_____

_____

_____

> In an *aristocracy*, a class of noblemen rule (Greek base *arist(o)-* = "best"). An *aristocrat* is a member of the ruling class or nobility. *Aristocrats* "believe in rule by" the "best"—themselves! They believe that their wealth and family position make them the best people to rule. In ancient Greece, the first form of government was an *aristocracy*. Power was held by *aristocrats* whose families had owned large tracts of land for several generations. Over time, the Greeks of Athens developed *democracy*, a system that gave power to the citizens, who would assemble and vote for their leaders. The Greeks believed that *democracy* was a better form of government than an *aristocracy*, and even better than a *monarchy*.

◎ Do you agree with the Ancient Greeks that a *democracy* is best? Why or why not?

_____

_____

Name: _____   Date: _____

About the Root: Government:
What Is an Autocracy?

Directions: Read the information. Then answer the question.

Autocracy is rule by one person. It is the opposite of *democracy*, which is rule by the people. Dictatorships are autocracies. *Autocrats* have unlimited power, authority, and influence. They can make all decisions. It does not matter if others do not like them or their rules.

Autocracy seems as if it could be harmful. But *autocratic* leadership is sometimes needed. In dangerous situations, where there is little room for error, rigid rules can keep people safe. Some believe the United States military uses an *autocratic* leadership style.

◎ Can you think of any situation in which an autocratic ruler might be a good idea for a short period of time?

_____

_____

_____

_____

_____

_____

Name: _____ Date: _____

About the Root: Government:
What Is a Bureaucracy?

. . . .

Directions: Read the information. Then answer the question.

A *bureau* (French word) is a cabinet with many drawers for storage. This word originally described a writing desk with many small compartments and pigeonholes. A *bureau* is also a government office. A leader who works with a bureau, sometimes called a cabinet, divides the duties of governing into several small "compartments." The result is a complex *bureaucracy* (which means "rule by the cabinet").

Bureaucrats work in a bureaucracy. Because a *bureaucracy* often contains a tangled network of "red tape" upheld by bureaucrats, these words can be pejorative or derogatory. Petty bureaucrats watch over their tiny compartments and slavishly follow rules. The phrase *government bureaucracy* usually refers to inefficiency. Too many compartments make it difficult to get things done. Think of a huge desk with so many drawers that you don't know which one to open first!

◎ Why do you think that *bureaucracy* and other words related to it have such negative meanings?

_____

_____

_____

_____

Name: _____ Date: _____

Divide and Conquer:
Who Is the Ruler?

Directions: Use the Base/Prefix Bank to help you identify the roots of the words below. Write the letter from the Definition Bank for the correct word.

Base/Prefix Bank

arist(o)- = "the best"   *dem(o)-* = "the people"   *the(o)-* = "God"
auto- = "self"   *plut(o)-* = "wealth," "wealthy"

Definition Bank

A. a person, such as a nobleman, who believes that his privileged birth qualifies him for office

B. government by the rich

C. "government of the people, by the people, for the people" (the words of Abraham Lincoln)

D. a state run by religious teachings and sacred texts

E. dictatorial monarch

Word	First Base/ Prefix Means	Second Base/ Suffix Means	Definition
1. plutocracy			
2. aristocrat			
3. theocracy			
4. democracy			
5. autocrat			

Base -*crat*, -*cracy*

Name: _____ Date: _____

Making Connections:
Who/What Am I?

Directions: Match each word in the first column with its speaker in the second column.

Word	Speaker
_____ 1. bureaucracy	**A.** I am a person in charge of a small office and insist that people seek my approval before proceeding.
_____ 2. gynecocracy	**B.** I am a stern dictator.
_____ 3. aristocrat	**C.** I believe that our country's laws should be based on a set of religious beliefs.
_____ 4. plutocrat	**D.** I am the maze of government offices that make it hard to get anything done.
_____ 5. bureaucrat	**E.** I am a government in which women have all the power.
_____ 6. autocrat	**F.** I was born into a noble family with a lot of property and think that people like me make the best rulers.
_____ 7. theocrat	**G.** I believe that people who make or have a lot of money deserve to control the government.

You Try It! Use one of the words *bureaucratic, autocratic,* or *democratic* in a sentence.

_____

_____

_____

_____

_____

_____

Base *dic-, dict-*

dic-, dict- = "say," "speak," "tell"

Standards

Uses common, grade-appropriate Greek or Latin affixes and roots as clues to the meaning of a word

Determines the meaning of words and phrases as they are used in a text, including vocabulary specific to domains related to history/social studies

By the end of the year, reads and comprehends literary nonfiction in the grades 6–8 text complexity band proficiently, with scaffolding as needed at the high end of the range

Materials

- *About the Root: World History: What Is a Dictator?* (page 38)

- *About the Root: Government: Dict- in the Law* (page 39)

- *About the Root: World History: What Was the Edict of Milan?* (page 40)

- *Divide and Conquer: Saying, Speaking, Telling* (page 41)

- *Making Connections: Who/What Am I?* (page 42)

Teacher Preparation

- Read and review the background information about the base *dic-*, *dict-* on page 37 to familiarize yourself with its context in social studies and government.

- Read and review the glossary of the base found on the Digital Resource CD (filename: rootsglossary.pdf) for additional support.

Guided Practice

About the Root

1. Distribute copies of pages 38, 39, and/or 40 to students. Now write *dic-, dict-* on the board. Tell students that these bases mean "say," "speak," or "tell." Have students think about words with this root. After a few minutes, invite sharing.

2. Have students read the passages and answer the questions. Students can work independently or with partners. You may want to conclude with a whole-class discussion to review students' answers and reinforce the meaning of the roots in context.

Divide and Conquer

3. Distribute copies of *Divide and Conquer* (page 41). As you guide students through the activity page, use questions like these to generate discussion about each of the words:

   - Where is the meaning of "say," "speak," or "tell" in the word _____?

   - Where might you see the word _____?

   - Can you think of an example of _____?

Base *dic-, dict-* *(cont.)*

Making Connections

4. Distribute copies of *Making Connections* (page 42).

5. Have students read all of the definitions before completing the activity sheet.

6. Conclude with a whole-class discussion that focuses on root meaning. You might invite whole-class brainstorming of *dic-, dict-* words. Or you could ask pairs of students to select a couple of words from the list and develop lists of related words from them (e.g., *abdication: abdicate, abdicated,* or *abdicating*).

Words with *dic-, dict-*

abdicate	diction
abdication	dictionary
addict	dictum
addiction	edict
addictive	indicate
benediction	indication
contradict	indicator
contradiction	indict
contradictory	indictment
dedicate	jurisdiction
dedication	malediction
dedicatory	predict
dictate	prediction
dictator	predictive
dictatorial	verdict
dictatorship	valedictorian

A list of words to print out for students can be found on the Digital Resource CD (filename: wordlists.pdf).

Teacher Background Information and Tips

Base *dic-*, *dict-* = "say," "speak," "tell"

The Latin base *dic-*, *dict-* means "say," "speak," "tell" and appears in many words in social studies. As suggested by the expression "to have the final *say,*" the base *dic-*, *dict-* refers to authoritative speech. A *dictator* tells subjects what to do by *dictating* the rules from a position of authority. When we take *dictation*, we write down every word spoken by the authorized speaker. A *dictionary* contains only the authorized words in a language as officially recognized by language authorities. The word *dedicate* is also built on the base *dic-*. When we *dedicate* a monument, we make a public and formal declaration expressed in spoken words.

The authoritative sense of this base is especially strong in the words *jurisdiction*, *verdict*, and *indict*.

This base also refers to "formal speech," such as declarations. An *edict* is a formal proclamation by a ruler; a *valedictorian* gives the farewell speech at a graduation ceremony; a cleric delivers a *benediction* at the end of a ceremony; and when we practice our *diction*, we practice our formal delivery and oral expression of words.

Important social studies words built on this base include *dictator, abdicate, edict, jurisdiction, and indict*.

For a glossary of words with this root, see the Digital Resource CD (filename: rootsglossary.pdf).

Base *dic-*, *dict-*

Name: _____   Date: _____

About the Root: World History:
What Is a Dictator?

Directions: Read the information. Then answer the questions.

> The Latin base *dic-*, *dict-* means "say," "speak," "tell." Because this base often refers to people who have the final "say" in a situation, it can describe rulers and governments. Think of such expressions as "Because I *say* so" and "I'm *telling* you to do this," and you will have a good understanding of what this Latin base means.

Use the meaning of the base to explain these words:

◎ predict (*pre-* means "before")

_____

◎ verdict (the Latin base *ver-* means "truth")

_____

> A *dictator* is a ruler who has total control over a country. A dictator simply declares "Because I *say* so" as the reason for decisions. Other people must slavishly follow these *dictates* or face dreadful penalties.
>
> *Dictators* have sole and absolute power. They usually limit civil freedoms. They may repress their rivals. Sometimes, dictators also control the military.
>
> Most of us know Adolph Hitler as a dictator in Germany during World War II. Some countries have dictators even today. Kim Jong-Il was a dictator in North Korea. *Parade* magazine recently named his rule "the world's most repressive regime."

◎ The word *dictator* has a negative tone. Why do you think this is so?

_____

_____

◎ The word *dictator* is built on the same base as the word *verdict*. How do the words *dictator* and *verdict* both mean "say," or "tell"?

_____

_____

_____

Name: _____

Date: _____

About the Root: Government:
Dict- in the Law

Directions: Read the information. Then answer the questions.

If you think about the meaning of *dict-*, it makes sense that it would be found in words about law. If a court has *jurisdiction* (Latin base *jur[is]* = law), it has power to explain (or "speak") the law. A suspect must be officially *indicted* (pronounced: in-DI-ted) for a trial to begin. An *indictment* (pronounced: in-DITE-ment) is a formal charge that is "spoken," "declared on" the suspect. At the end of the trial, the judge or jury renders a final *verdict*.

◎ Why do you think so many legal words are based on *dict-*?

_____

_____

_____

_____

_____

◎ Think about the word *verdict*. If the Latin base *ver-* means "true, truth," can you describe what a *verdict* is?

_____

_____

_____

_____

_____

Name: _____   Date: _____

About the Root: World History:
What Was the Edict of Milan?

Directions: Read the information. Then answer the question.

An important year in the history of religious tolerance was 313 A.D. Early Christians refused to worship the many gods of Rome. So the Romans arrested, tortured, and killed them. But in 313, in the Italian city of Milan, the Emperor Constantine issued an *edict*. It was openly declared to all members of the Roman Empire. This is called the *Edict of Milan*. It stated, "We command …that Christians and non-Christians alike should be allowed to keep the faith of their own religious beliefs and worship" (Eusebius 1989, 322). The Edict of Milan legalized Christianity as a religion. It also allowed other people to worship as they saw fit.

◎ In 1863, an edict called the *Emancipation Proclamation* ended slavery in the United States. Compare the *Emancipation Proclamation* and the *Edict of Milan*. How are the two edicts similar? How are they different?

_____

_____

_____

_____

_____

_____

_____

Name: _____ Date: _____

Divide and Conquer:
Saying, Speaking, Telling

Directions: Use the Base/Prefix Bank to help you identify the roots of the words below. Write the letter from the Definition Bank for the correct word.

Base/Prefix Bank

ab- = "away," "from"   *jur(is)-* = "law"

in- = "in," "on," "into"   *ver-* = "true," "truth"

Definition Bank

A. an official or formal charge or accusation

B. an autocrat

C. a final decision rendered by a judge or jury

D. the authority to interpret or apply a law or to decide a case

E. to renounce power or position

Word	First Base/ Prefix Means	Second Base/ Suffix Means	Definition
1. verdict			
2. dictator		*-ator* = one who (does)	
3. indictment			
4. jurisdiction			
5. abdicate			

Name: _____   Date: _____

Making Connections:
Who/What Am I?

. . . .

Directions: Match each word on the left with a definition/context on the right. Put the number of the answer in the Magic Square Box. If you are correct, each row and column will add up to the same number. (**Hint:** You will not use one of the words.)

Word		Speaker
_____ **A.** indictment		**1.** I mean to point out something.
_____ **B.** dictatorship		**2.** I am the regime overseen by a tyrant.
_____ **C.** verdict		**3.** I am the right or power to make legal decisions.
_____ **D.** benediction		**4.** I am the closing prayer of blessing delivered at the end of a service or ceremony.
_____ **E.** edict		**5.** I mean to say the opposite of what someone else says.
_____ **F.** abdication		**6.** I am an official decree uttered by a ruler declaring a policy.
_____ **G.** contradict		**7.** I am the final decision on whether the defendant is guilty or innocent.
_____ **H.** dictator		**8.** I am the renunciation of power and position, enacted when a monarch steps down from the throne.
_____ **I.** jurisdiction		**9.** I am a formal charge brought against a suspect for a crime.
_____ **J.** indicate		**10.** I am someone who takes political power by force.

A:	B:	C:
D:	E:	F:
G:	H:	I:

Magic Number:

_____

Base *judg-, judic-*

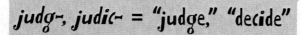

judg-, judic- = "judge," "decide"

Standards

Uses common, grade-appropriate Greek or Latin affixes and roots as clues to the meaning of a word

Determines the meaning of words and phrases as they are used in a text, including vocabulary specific to domains related to history/social studies

By the end of the year, reads and comprehends literary nonfiction in the grades 6–8 text complexity band proficiently, with scaffolding as needed at the high end of the range

Materials

- *About the Root: Government: The Supreme Court* (page 46)

- *About the Root: Culture and Society: Prejudice* (page 47)

- *About the Root: Government: Sub Judice* (page 48)

- *Divide and Conquer: You Be the Judge* (page 49)

- *Making Connections: Complete the Sentence* (page 50)

Teacher Preparation

- Read and review the background information about the base *judg-, judic-* on page 45 to familiarize yourself with their context in culture, society, and government.

- Read and review the glossary of the base found on the Digital Resource CD (filename: rootsglossary.pdf) for additional support.

Guided Practice

About the Root

1. Write *judg-* and *judic-* on the board. Ask students to guess what the base means. As students offer ideas, ask them to share reasons for these definitions. Then put students into groups of two or three. Give groups two minutes to brainstorm as many words containing *judg-* or *judic-* as they can. Conclude with whole-group sharing. You may want to create a class list to post.

2. Distribute copies of pages 46, 47, and/or 48 to students. Have them read the passages and answer the questions. Students can work independently or with partners. You may want to conclude with a whole-class discussion to review students' answers and reinforce the meaning of the roots in context.

Base judg-, judic- (cont.)

Divide and Conquer

3. Distribute copies of *Divide and Conquer* (page 49). As you guide students through the activity page, use questions like these to generate discussion about each of the words:

- Where is the meaning of "judge" or "decide" in the word _____?

- Where might you see the word _____?

- Can you think of an example of _____?

Making Connections

4. Distribute copies of *Making Connections* (page 50).

5. Have students preview all of the sentences before completing the activity sheet.

6. Conclude this activity with a whole-class discussion that focuses on root meaning. You might invite pairs of students to rewrite sentences 1 and 2 so that the answers are the opposite of what they originally were (e.g., rewrite sentence #1 so the answer is *judicious*).

Words with judg-, judic-

adjudicate

injudicious

judge

judgment

judgmental

judicial

judiciary

judicious

misjudge

misjudgment

nonjudgmental

nonprejudiced

prejudge

prejudice

prejudiced

prejudicial

sub judice

A list of words to print out for students can be found on the Digital Resource CD (filename: wordlists.pdf).

Teacher Background Information and Tips

Base *judg-*, *judic-* = "judge," "decide"

The Latin base *judg-*, *judic-* means "judge," "decide" and appears in many words in social studies, especially in the context of the United States government. The Constitution establishes three branches of government: executive (Article One), legislative (Article Two), and *judicial* (Article Three). Also called the *judiciary*, the *judicial* branch consists of the Supreme Court and lower courts. The essential function of the *judiciary* is contained in the base *judg-*, *judic-*. This branch "judges" cases regarding interpretations of the law and renders decisions on guilt or innocence in cases of crimes.

Important social studies words that are built on this base include *judge*, *judicial*, *prejudice*, and *judicious*.

For a glossary of words with this root, see the Digital Resource CD (filename: rootsglossary.pdf).

Name: _____   Date: _____

About the Root: Government:
The Supreme Court

. . . .

Directions: Read the information. Then answer the questions.

> The Latin bases *judg-* and *judic-* means "judge," "decide." They appear in many social studies words. You probably already know words built with this base. Answer these questions:

◎ Who is the head of a courtroom? _____

◎ A *judicious* decision shows intelligence and good judgment. Give an example of an *injudicious* decision.

_____

_____

_____

> Article III of the United States Constitution established the judicial branch but left Congress to define its shape and structure. Even the number of supreme court justices is left to Congress. At times in our history, there have been as few as six justices. Since 1869, we have had nine supreme court justices, one chief justice, and eight associate justices.
>
> Citizens elect the president and members of Congress, but members of the judicial branch are appointed. The president nominates a potential supreme court justice, for example, and the Senate confirms him or her. Supreme court justices generally serve until their retirement or death. They can be removed from office through impeachment. The House of Representatives could impeach a justice, and the Senate could convict him or her. Only one supreme court justice, Samuel Chase, was ever impeached. The Senate did not convict him, however, and Justice Chase continued on the court until his death in 1811.

◎ Why do you think the framers of the Constitution decided that supreme court justices should be appointed rather than elected?

_____

_____

_____

Name: _____   Date: _____

About the Root:
Culture and Society: Prejudice

Directions: Read the information. Then answer the question.

Every once in a while, we hear people making negative comments about others. Sometimes, these comments are *prejudiced*. A *prejudice* is an unfavorable opinion or "judgment" formed "before" learning all the facts.

Prejudices are not only foolish and irrational but they can also be dangerous. Some people are unfairly *prejudiced* against others simply based on the color of their skin, the name of their religion, their sex, or even the amount of money they have or do not have!

In July 2011, results of a national poll about prejudice were released. Some responses were puzzling. For example, 67 percent of the more than 10,000 people who responded said they themselves would not care about the race of a convenience store clerk. Although they said they were not prejudiced, 71 percent of these same respondents said "most Americans'" first choice would be a white clerk.

◎ Do you think most people are *prejudiced* in some way? Explain your thinking.

_____

_____

_____

_____

_____

Name: _____   Date: _____

About the Root: Government:
Sub Judice

Directions: Read the information. Then answer the questions.

The two-word Latin phrase *sub judice*, (pronounced sub JOO-dee-keh or sub YOO-dee-keh) means "under a judge." Think of a judge, seated high on the bench and holding a gavel. Because the judge holds the highest position in the courtroom, everything takes place "under" him or her. So, when a trial is in progress and a verdict has not yet been reached, we say that the case is *sub judice.* This saying gives rise to the expression, "I'll place that *under judgment*." Whenever we say that, we mean, "I'll think about it, but I have not yet made up my mind."

◎ Judges are often seated above the rest of the people in a courtroom. Why do you think this is so?

_____

_____

_____

◎ What are some aspects of a trial that the judge controls?

_____

_____

_____

Name: _____ Date: _____

Divide and Conquer:
You Be the Judge

Directions: Use the Base/Prefix Bank to help you identify the roots of the words below. Write the letter from the Definition Bank for the correct word.

Base/Prefix Bank

ad- = "to," "toward," "add to"   *in-* = "not"   *pre-* = "before"

Definition Bank

A. unwise, foolish, showing poor judgment

B. preside over a trial; sit in judgment over

C. biased or bigoted

D. sound and wise; showing good judgment

E. pertaining to courts of law

Word	First Base/ Prefix Means	Second Base/ Suffix Means	Definition
1. judicious		*-ious* = full of	
2. adjudicate			
3. prejudiced			
4. judicial		*-ial* = of, like, related to	
5. injudicious			

Name: _____   Date: _____

Making Connections:
Complete the Sentence

Directions: Use the words in the Word Bank to complete the sentences below.

Word Bank

| adjudicated | injudicious | judicial | misjudged | prejudice |

1. It was _____ of me to watch so much television on Sunday. I had a big test on Monday!

2. I want to apologize. I think I _____ you when I accused you of taking my coat on purpose.

3. One of the best ways to overcome ethnic and cultural _____ is to study foreign cultures and spend time with people who are not exactly like you.

4. This trial will be _____ by a new judge who has just arrived in our district.

5. Do you think that all decisions rendered by our _____ system are fair and sound?

You Try It!

Make a fill-in-the-blank sentence for each word below. Ask your partner to fill in the blanks.

judgmental

_____

judicious

_____

judiciary

_____

Bases *popul-* and *dem(o)-*

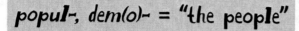

popul-, dem(o)- = "the people"

Standards

Uses common, grade-appropriate Greek or Latin affixes and roots as clues to the meaning of a word

Determines the meaning of words and phrases as they are used in a text, including vocabulary specific to domains related to history/social studies

By the end of the year, reads and comprehends literary nonfiction in the grades 6–8 text complexity band proficiently, with scaffolding as needed at the high end of the range

Materials

- *About the Root: American History: What Difference Does the "The" Make?* (page 54)

- *About the Root: Civics: What Is a Populist?* (page 55)

- *About the Root: What Are Demographics?* (page 56)

- *Divide and Conquer: Of, By, and For the People* (page 57)

- *Making Connections: Riddles* (page 58)

Teacher Preparation

- Read and review the background information about the bases *popul-* and *dem(o)-* on page 53 to familiarize yourself with their context in history, civics, and government.

- Read and review the glossary of the bases found on the Digital Resource CD (filename: rootsglossary.pdf) for additional support.

Guided Practice

About the Root

1. Distribute copies of pages 54, 55, and/or 56 to students. Write *popul-* and *dem(o)-* on the board. Tell students that these bases mean "the people." Ask pairs of students to think about words they already know with these bases. Conclude with whole-group sharing.

2. Have students read the passages and answer the questions. Students can work independently or with partners. You may want to conclude with a whole-class discussion to review students' answers and reinforce the meaning of the roots in context.

Divide and Conquer

3. Distribute copies of *Divide and Conquer* (page 57). As you guide students through the activity page, use questions like these to generate discussion about each of the words:

   - Where is the meaning of the "people" in the word _____?

   - Where might you see the word _____?

   - Can you think of an example of _____?

Bases *popul-* and *dem(o)-* (cont.)

Making Connections

4. Distribute copies of *Making Connections* (page 58).

5. You may want to develop a sample riddle to model with students before they complete the activity sheet. After students have written their own riddles, they may want partners to try to solve them.

6. Conclude with a whole-class discussion that focuses on root meaning.

Words with dem(o)-, and popul- = "the people"

demagogue
demagoguery
democracy
democract
democratic
demographics
demography
depopulate
epidemic
pandemic
populace
popular
popularity
populate
population
populist
populism
populous
repopulate
undemocratic
unpopular

A list of words to print out for students can be found on the Digital Resource CD (filename: wordlists.pdf).

Teacher Background Information and Tips

Bases *popul-* and *dem(o)-* = "the people"

The Latin base *popul-* and the Greek base *dem(o)-* mean "the people" and appear in many words in social studies. Because these bases refer to "the people" as a collective and not as individuals, they provide the base meaning of many words dealing with communities, population groups, and society at large.

The Latin base *popul-* is found in many general words that students may already know. *Popular* music, for example, appeals to a large number of "people." The number of "people" in an area makes up its *population*. A *populous* state (such as California) has a large number of "people" living in it. The masses, or so-called "common people," are referred to as the general *populace*, as differentiated from the affluent or elite. The words *populace* and *populous* are homophones: they are spelled differently but have the same pronunciation.

As a Greek base, *dem(o)-* is found in words of a more technical nature. An *epidemic*, for example, is a disease or outbreak that falls "upon" (Greek prefix *epi-* = "on," "upon") "the people" by spreading quickly over a large area. When the disease affects nearly "all" the population, it becomes a *pandemic* (Greek prefix *pan-* = "all"). A *demagogue* is a public leader (Greek base *agog-* = "lead") who exploits the fears, superstitions, and prejudices of large groups of "people" by rousing their emotions. *Demographics* is the study of populations according to their size, density, and vital statistics. *Demographic* reports are often published as graphs and tables. This is why the base *graph-* is used in the suffix (Greek base *graph-* = "write," "draw").

Important social studies words that are built on these bases include *populism*, *populous*, *democracy*, *pandemic*, and *demagogue*.

For a glossary of words with these roots, see the Digital Resource CD (filename: rootsglossary.pdf).

Name: _____   Date: _____

About the Root: American History:
What Difference Does the "The" Make?

Directions: Read the information. Then answer the questions.

> The Latin base *popul-* and the Greek base *dem(o)-* mean "the people." These bases refer to "the people" as a group, not as individuals. They provide the base meaning of many words dealing with communities, population groups, and society at large. Work with a partner to answer these questions.

◎ How does the base *popul-* help define what *popular* music is?

_____

_____

◎ What do we mean when we say that California is a *populous* state?

_____

_____

◎ *Epi-* means "on," "upon." Use this to explain the meaning of *epidemic*.

_____

_____

_____

> On November 19, 1863, President Abraham Lincoln gave a two-minute speech that showed the soul of the democratic spirit. The Civil War was raging. He spoke at the opening of a national cemetery in Gettysburg, Pennsylvania. At this battle site, more than 5,000 soldiers had been killed and over 17,000 wounded.
>
> In his Gettysburg Address, the president wanted to honor the fallen soldiers. He said, "We here highly resolve that these dead shall not have died in vain. That this nation, under God, shall have a new birth of freedom. And that government *of the people, by the people, for the people,* shall not perish from the earth." By saying *the people,* he brought the country together. Saying "Government of people, by people, and for people" would have sent a much different message. But by adding *the* to *people,* he described democracy.

◎ Explain the difference between *people* and *the people* on a separate sheet of paper.

Name: _____   Date: _____

About the Root: Civics:
What Is a Populist?

Directions: Read the information. Then answer the question.

The word *populist* literally means "one who believes in the people." In the late 1800s, American farmers and workers started a new political party, The People's Party. Their members came to be known as *Populists*. Populists wanted to improve people's lives. For example, they wanted a graduated income tax. They thought this would spread out the costs of government more fairly. They also wanted an eight-hour limit to the workday. And they asked for a nationalized railroad system to make transportation cheaper.

Most people did not like these ideas. People thought they were too revolutionary. They were afraid that the Populist ideas would destroy democracy.

The Populist Party was founded in 1891 and disbanded in 1908. Its legacy, however, was lasting. Nearly all Populist ideas have become law. Today, whenever a political candidate supports the causes of the populace, he or she is still called a *populist*.

◎ If the Populist Party were active today, what causes might it support? Explain your thinking.

_____

_____

_____

_____

_____

_____

_____

_____

_____

Name: _____ Date: _____

About the Root:
What Are Demographics?

Directions: Read the information. Then answer the question.

The term *demographics* is found in social studies. Demographic studies examine the makeup of a population according to statistics. In conducting demographic studies, researchers may organize people by gender, age, education, employment, household income, and ethnicity. Researchers often display their findings in pie charts. These show the percentages of people in a specific geographic area who, for example, hold high school diplomas, college degrees, graduate degrees, and professional licenses.

The word *demographics* perfectly describes these pie charts: the Greek base *dem(o)-* means "people" as a group, and the Greek base *graph-* means "write," "draw." Thus, a demographic chart is a "drawing of the people" according to the various criteria that demographers measure.

◎ Talk to a partner. Why would social scientists be interested in the demographics of an area?

_____

_____

_____

_____

_____

_____

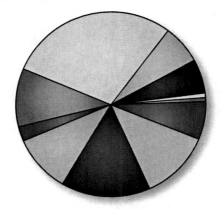

Name: _____ Date: _____

Divide and Conquer:

Of, By, and For the People

Directions: Use the Base/Prefix Bank to help you identify the roots of the words below. Write the letter from the Definition Bank for the correct word.

Base/Prefix Bank

crat- = "ruler"   *epi-* = "on," "upon"   *graph-* = "write," "draw"

Definition Bank

A. a disease affecting a large portion of the population in an area

B. a political philosophy promoting the interests of the common people

C. favoring government of, by, and for the people

D. having a high concentration of people; having a large population

E. statistical studies of population groups

Word	First Base/ Prefix Means	Second Base/ Suffix Means	Definition
1. demographics			
2. populism		*-ism* = belief in	
3. democratic			
4. epidemic			
5. populous		*-ous* = full of	

Name: _____   Date: _____

Making Connections:
Riddles

. . . .

Directions: Solve each riddle with a word that contains *popul-* or *dem(o)-*. Then create your own to share with a partner.

---

1. I am a noun.

   I have four syllables.

   I have two roots.

   One root means "the people."

   The other root means "rule by."

   I am a form of government invented by the ancient Greeks.

   What am I?

   _____

2. I am a noun.

   I have four syllables.

   I have two roots.

   One root means "upon."

   The other root means "the people."

   A bad flu outbreak is an example of me.

   What am I?

   _____

3. I am a noun.

   I have three syllables.

   I have a Latin base that means "the people."

   I have a suffix that means "one who."

   I am a person who advocates policies that improve the lives of all the people.

   What am I?

   _____

You Try It!

Write your own riddles for two of the following words on a separate sheet of paper: *demographics, popular, population.*

Bases urb-, urban- and poli-, -polis

urb-, urban-, poli-, -polis = "city"

Standards

Uses common, grade-appropriate Greek or Latin affixes and roots as clues to the meaning of a word

Determines the meaning of words and phrases as they are used in a text, including vocabulary specific to domains related to history/social studies

By the end of the year, reads and comprehends literary nonfiction in the grades 6–8 text complexity band proficiently, with scaffolding as needed at the high end of the range

Materials

- *About the Root: Civics: Man Is a Political Animal* (page 62)

- *About the Root: Ancient History: Citizenship: A True Story* (page 63)

- *About the Root: City Matters: Phrases that Employ the Word* Urban (page 64)

- *Divide and Conquer: City Living* (page 65)

- *Making Connections: Who/What Am I?* (page 66)

Teacher Preparation

- Read and review the background information about the bases *urb-*, *urban-* and *poli-*, *-polis* on page 61 to familiarize yourself with their context in social studies and civics.

- Read and review the glossary of the bases found on the Digital Resource CD (filename: rootsglossary.pdf) for additional support.

Guided Practice

About the Root

1. Distribute copies of pages 62, 63, and/or 64 to students. Write *urb-*, *urban-*, *poli-*, and *-polis* on the board. Tell students that these bases mean "city." Ask pairs of students to think about words they already know with these roots. Invite whole-group sharing.

2. Have students read the passages and answer the questions. Students can work independently or with partners. You may want to conclude with a whole-class discussion to review students' answers and reinforce the meaning of the roots in context.

Divide and Conquer

3. Distribute copies of *Divide and Conquer* (page 65). As you guide students through the activity page, use questions like these to generate discussion about each of the words:

   - Where is the meaning of "city" in the word _____?

   - Where might you see the word _____?

   - Can you think of an example of _____?

Bases urb-, urban- and poli-, -polis (cont.)

Making Connections

4. Distribute copies of *Making Connections* (page 66).

5. Have students read all of the definitions before completing the activity sheet.

6. Conclude with a whole-class discussion that focuses on root meaning. Stress the concept of "city" as you discuss items.

Words with urb-, urban-, and poli-, -polis

acropolis
Annapolis
apolitical
cosmopolitan
cosmopolite
exurbs
Indianapolis
megalopolis
metropolis
metropolitan
Minneapolis
necropolis
police
policy
polis
politic
political
politics
urban
urbane
urbanity
interurban
inurbane
suburban
suburbs

A list of words to print out for students can be found on the Digital Resource CD (filename: wordlists.pdf).

Teacher Background Information and Tips

Bases *urb-*, *urban-* and *poli-*, *-polis* = "city"

The Latin base *urb-*, *urban-* and the Greek base *poli-*, *-polis* mean "city." These bases appear in many social studies words referring to cities as places (e.g., *urban, suburbs, acropolis, metropolitan*) and to the people living and working in them (e.g., *suburbanites, politicians, police*). The Latin base *urb-*, *urban-* conveys both the idea of "city" as a dwelling place and the characteristics associated with city living. Important social studies words built on this Latin base include *urban, urbanize, suburbs,* and *urbanity*.

The Greek base *poli-*, *-polis* is frequently attached to a Greek base by a connecting *o*, resulting in these words: *acropolis, cosmopolitan,* and *necropolis*.

For a glossary of words with these roots, see the Digital Resource CD (filename: rootsglossary.pdf).

Note: the word *polite* is not from the Greek base *poli-*. It is from Latin *poli-*, which means "to polish," "to smooth." A polite person, therefore has "smooth and polished manners." The word has nothing to do with "city refinements."

Name: _____   Date: _____

About the Root: Civics:
Man Is a Political Animal

Directions: Read the information. Then answer the questions.

> The Latin base *urb-, urban-* and the Greek base *poli-, -polis* mean "city." These bases appear in many social studies words that refer to cities as physical places (e.g., *urban, suburbs, acropolis, metropolitan*) and to the people who live and work in them (e.g., *suburbanites, politicians, police*).

◎ Work with a partner. Select three words in parentheses above. Explain how the meaning of each has to do with the city.

_____

_____

_____

_____

> Aristotle was an ancient Greek philosopher. He said, "Man is by nature a *political* animal. He who is without a state or city is...tribeless and lawless." Aristotle thought that people naturally lived in social communities called *poleis*, or "city-states." People could perfect themselves by living together and establishing laws and manners. This would make life better for everyone. As individuals tried to control the ancient city of Athens, the science of *politics* emerged, along with *politicians*. Today, *politics* can refer to state, national, and even international issues. But *political* science began in the ancient Greek city-state.

◎ Do you agree with Aristotle? Are people political by nature? Explain your thinking.

_____

_____

_____

_____

_____

_____

_____

Name: _____ Date: _____

About the Root: Ancient History:
Citizenship: A True Story

Directions: Read the information. Then answer the questions.

The ancient Greeks did not have last names. They used their first names, followed by their fathers' name and then the name of their city. The famous philosopher Socrates, for example, was "Socrates, son of Sophroniscus, from Athens."

But Socrates did not view himself as only a citizen of Athens. He wanted to understand what truth and justice meant for everyone. So he called himself "a citizen of the world." The Greek word for "world" is *cosmos.* Although he walked through Athens barefoot in ragged clothes and paid no attention to high fashion, Socrates claimed to be *cosmopolitan*!

Today, the word *cosmopolitan* makes us think of gracious living. But the ancient historian Plutarch explained, "When you are a *cosmopolite* (a person who is *cosmopolitan*) there are no boundaries to your native land. You breathe the same air and drink the same water as all the world. Because the same laws preside over everyone, you uphold the justice that is due to all human beings as your fellow citizens."

◎ Do you agree with Plutarch's idea that all human beings are our fellow citizens? Why or why not?

_____

_____

_____

◎ If he were alive today, do you think Socrates would still consider himself a *cosmopolitan*? Why or why not?

_____

_____

_____

Name: _____   Date: _____

About the Root: City Matters:
Phrases that Employ the Word Urban

Directions: Read the information. Then answer the question.

The Latin base *urb-, urban-* refers to "the city" as a physical space. People who live an *urban* lifestyle may live in apartment buildings. They have easy access to public transportation. But people who live in the *suburbs* usually need their own transportation to go to work or do their shopping. Below are some phrases that include the word *urban*.

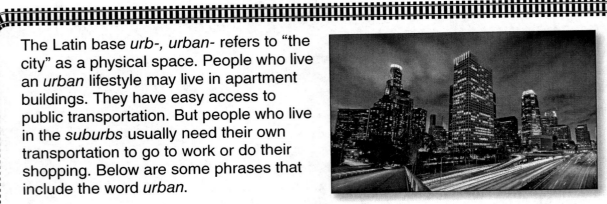

Select two of the following phrases. Tell how the meaning of each one has to do with the "city."

◎ *Urban* planning   ◎ *Urban* sprawl

◎ *Urban* renewal   ◎ *Urban* decay

Phrase 1:

_____

_____

_____

_____

_____

Phrase 2:

_____

_____

_____

_____

_____

Name: _____   Date: _____

Divide and Conquer:
City Living

Directions: Use the Base/Prefix Bank to help you identify the roots of the words below. Write the letter from the Definition Bank for the correct word.

Base/Prefix Bank

acro- = "high," "top"   *inter-* = "between"   *sub-* = "under," "below"
cosm(o)- = "world"   *megal(o)-* = "big," "large"

Definition Bank

A. connecting two or more cities or urban areas

B. sophisticated; having worldly tastes and refinement

C. the citadel or fortified high part of an ancient city

D. a very large city or urban area

E. one who dwells in an area close to but not within a city

Word	First Base/ Prefix Means	Second Base/ Suffix Means	Definition
1. megalopolis			
2. interurban			
3. cosmopolitan			
4. acropolis			
5. suburbanite			

Name: _____   Date: _____

Making Connections:
Who/What Am I?

. . . .

Directions: Match each word or phrase in the first column with its speaker in the second column.

Word/Phrase	Speaker
_____ 1. greater metropolitan area	**A.** I am the high fortress overlooking ancient Athens.
_____ 2. urban blight	**B.** I am the large region encompassing the mother city and the surrounding suburbs and exurbs.
_____ 3. urban renewal	**C.** I am the study of government and politicians.
_____ 4. suburban lifestyle	**D.** I am the renovation of an old city.
_____ 5. Athenian Acropolis	**E.** I am the decay of a city, marked by abandoned and dilapidated buildings.
_____ 6. political science	**F.** I am the way people live outside the city limits.

You Try It!

Use one of the words *political, suburb,* or *megalopolis* in your own sentence:

_____

_____

_____

_____

_____

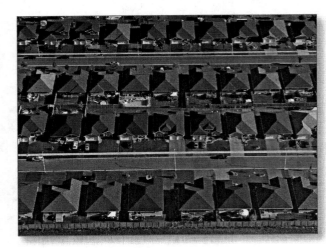

Bases civ-, cit-, civil- and milit-

civ-, cit-, civil- = "citizen"

milit- = "soldier," "fighter"

Standards

Uses common, grade-appropriate Greek or Latin affixes and roots as clues to the meaning of a word

Determines the meaning of words and phrases as they are used in a text, including vocabulary specific to domains related to history/social studies

By the end of the year, reads and comprehends literary nonfiction in the grades 6–8 text complexity band proficiently, with scaffolding as needed at the high end of the range

Materials

- *About the Root: Henry David Thoreau: A Lesson in Civics?* (page 70)

- *About the Root: Civics: Militant Women* (page 71)

- *About the Root: American History: Civil Rights* (page 72)

- *Divide and Conquer: Soldiers and Citizens* (page 73)

- *Making Connections: Word Sort* (page 74)

Teacher Preparation

- Read and review the background information about the bases *civ-, cit-, civil-* and *milit-* on page 69 to familiarize yourself with their context in history and civics.

- Read and review the glossary of the bases found on the Digital Resource CD (filename: rootsglossary.pdf) for additional support.

Guided Practice

About the Root

1. Distribute copies of pages 70, 71, and/or 72 to students. Ask partners to think about words they already know with these roots. After a few minutes, invite sharing.

2. Have students read the passages and answer the questions. Students can work independently or with partners. You may want to conclude with a whole-class discussion to review students' answers and reinforce the meaning of the roots in context.

Divide and Conquer

3. Distribute copies of *Divide and Conquer* (page 73). As you guide students through the activity page, use questions like these to generate discussion about each of the words:

   - Where is the meaning of "citizen," "soldier," or "fighter" in the word _____?

   - Where might you see the word _____?

   - Can you think of an example of _____?

Bases *civ-, cit-, civil-* and *milit-* (cont.)

Making Connections

4. Distribute copies of *Making Connections* (page 74).

5. Have students read carefully the headers in each section of the chart before they begin writing in the words and phrases.

6. Conclude with a whole-class discussion that focuses on root meaning.

Words with *civ-, cit-, civil-* and *milit-*

citadel
citizen
citiizenship
civics
civil
civil engineer
civil law
Civil Rights
civil servant
civil service
civil wedding
civilian
civilization
civilize
civilized
demilitarize
militant
militarize
militarized zone
militant
military
militate
militia
uncivil

A list of words to print out for students can be found on the Digital Resource CD (filename: wordlists.pdf).

Teacher Background Information and Tips

Bases *civ-*, *cit-*, *civil-* = "citizen" and *milit-* = "soldier," "fighter"

The Latin bases *civ-*, *cit-*, *civil-* mean "citizen," and the Latin base *milit-* means "soldier," "fighter." Most words built on *civ-*, *cit-*, *civil-* refer to "citizens" and the qualities associated with the *civilized* behavior and manners of a *civilization* (e.g., *civility*, *civil behavior*, *civil rights*, *civic duty*).

The Latin base *milit-* provides the root meaning of words associated with "soldiers" (e.g., to serve in the *military*) and with "fighting" for things (e.g., "to *militate* for social change" or "to express *militant* views"). Words based on *milit-* can also express ideas distinct from and even the opposite of the bases *civ-*, *cit-*, *civil-*. For example, a *military uniform* is distinct from *civilian clothes*. Soldiers no longer on official *military duty* are said to return to *civilian status*. In government, the *Civil Service* is separate from the Armed Services.

Important social studies words that are built on these bases include *civilization*, *civilian*, *citizen*, *militia*, *demilitarize*, and *militant*.

For a glossary of words with these roots, see the Digital Resource CD (filename: rootsglossary.pdf).

Name: _____   Date: _____

About the Root:

Henry David Thoreau: A Lesson in Civics?

Directions: Read the information. Then answer the questions.

> The Latin base *civ-*, *cit-*, *civil-* means "citizen." Most words built on *civ-*, *cit-*, *civil-* refer to "citizens" and the qualities of *civilized* behavior.
>
> The Latin base *milit-* means "soldier" or "fighter." It provides the root meaning of words about "soldiers" (e.g., to serve in the *military*). It also refers to "fighting" for things (e.g., "to *militate* for social change" or "to express *militant* views").

◎ Give an example of *civil* behavior.

_____

_____

◎ Give an example of a *militant* view.

_____

_____

◎ What does it mean "to *militate* for social change?"

_____

_____

> In 1849 the American writer Henry David Thoreau wrote an essay titled, "Civil Disobedience." Think about how strange this title sounds. When people are civil to one another, they are polite and respectful. How can one be civil and disobedient at the same time?
>
> Thoreau used this catchy title to draw attention to what he thought was an injustice. He was opposed to the Mexican War being waged at the time. He refused to pay the poll tax that raised money to fight the war. Thoreau thought that disobedience was his *civic* duty. He refused to fund the war because he did not believe in it. He thought that his disobedience was the *civil* thing to do!

◎ Do you think *civil disobedience* is ever a good idea? Why or why not? Write your thoughts on a separate sheet of paper.

Name: _____ Date: _____

About the Root: Civics:
Militant Women

Directions: Read the information. Then answer the questions.

For about 20 years following the American Revolution, women who lived in New Jersey could vote. In 1807, however, that changed—the right to vote was taken away from women. Shortly afterward, women began fighting for the right to vote. In 1848, a group of militant activists convened in Seneca Falls, New York. The Women's Suffrage movement continued until 1920. In that year, enough states ratified the 19th Amendment to the Constitution to make it law. The new law stated that states and the federal government could not restrict voting based on gender. Women could finally vote!

◎ It took more than 100 years for women to win the right to vote. Why do you think it took so long?

_____

_____

_____

_____

_____

_____

◎ Can you think of any other laws in American history that are the result of militant activism?

_____

_____

_____

_____

_____

Name: _____   Date: _____

About the Root: American History:
Civil Rights

Directions: Read the information. Then answer the question.

We usually think of Civil Rights as the fight for African-American equality that began in the 1950s. This is true, but our history includes other civil rights movements. For example, the Children's Rights Movement began in the 19th century. It focused on child labor and the plight of orphans. The Mexican American Civil Rights Movement began in the 1940s. Its goal was to empower Hispanics. The American Indian Movement is a Native American activist group that began in the late 1960s. Its goals focused on leadership and self-government.

Civil Rights movements are efforts to gain equality. They are usually political movements. Also, they are usually nonviolent. People often use civil resistance to persuade others.

◎ What are some similarities among groups fighting for civil rights?

_____

_____

_____

_____

_____

Name: _____   Date: _____

Divide and Conquer:
Soldiers and Citizens

Directions: Write a letter from the Definition Bank for each word.

Definition Bank

A. collected citizens standing ready to be called into armed service

B. to remove arms and soldiers from an area

C. one who acts aggressively to further a cause

D. a citizen not currently serving in the Armed Forces

E. a fortress

Word	First Base/ Prefix Means	Second Base/ Suffix Means	Definition
1. militant		X	
2. demilitarize	*de-* = down, off		
3. civilian		X	
4. militia		X	
5. citadel		*-del* = small (diminutive)	

Name: _____   Date: _____

Making Connections:
Word Sort

Directions: Put each of the words or phrases in the Word/Phrase Bank on the chart where they belong. Share your answers with a partner and explain your reasoning.

Word/Phrase Bank

civil	civil rights	civility	incivility	uncivilized
civil behavior	civil strife	civilized	uncivil	

Could describe a person	Could not describe a person
Positive word/phrase	**Negative word/phrase**
Person or idea	**Describing word**

Base sequ-, secut-

sequ-, secut- = "follow"

Standards

Uses common, grade-appropriate Greek or Latin affixes and roots as clues to the meaning of a word

Determines the meaning of words and phrases as they are used in a text, including vocabulary specific to domains related to history/social studies

By the end of the year, reads and comprehends literary nonfiction in the grades 6–8 text complexity band proficiently, with scaffolding as needed at the high end of the range

Materials

- *About the Root: Who/What Will You Follow?* (page 78)

- *About the Root: Civics: An Execution Sentence* (page 79)

- *About the Root: World History: Persecution* (page 80)

- *Divide and Conquer: Follow the Leader* (page 81)

- *Making Connections: Making Meaning* (page 82)

Teacher Preparation

- Read and review the background information about the base *sequ-*, *secut-* on page 77 to familiarize yourself with their context in civics and history.

- Read and review the glossary of the base found on the Digital Resource CD (filename: rootsglossary.pdf) for additional support.

Guided Practice

About the Root

1. Write *sequ-*, *secut-* on the board. Tell students that these bases mean "follow." Distribute copies of pages 78, 79, and/or 80 to students. Ask them to think about words they already know with this base. After a few minutes, invite sharing.

2. Have students read the passages and answer the questions. Students can work independently or with partners. You may want to conclude with a whole-class discussion to review students' answers and reinforce the meaning of the roots in context.

Divide and Conquer

3. Distribute copies of *Divide and Conquer* (page 81). As you guide students through the activity page, use questions like these to generate discussion about each of the words:

   - Where is the meaning of "follow" in the word _____?

   - Where might you see the word _____?

   - Can you think of an example of _____?

Base sequ-, secut- *(cont.)*

Making Connections

4. Distribute copies of *Making Connections* (page 82).

5. Encourage students to read the sentences on the activity page carefully and to use the context clues to help them understand the vocabulary.

6. Conclude with a whole-class discussion that focuses on root meaning. Focus on the use of "follow" in the sentences. You could also ask students to rewrite the sentences using "follow" instead of the italicized words/phrases.

Words with sequ-, secut-

consecutive
consequence
consequential
execute
execution
executioner
executive
executor
inconsequential
persecute
persecution
prosecute
prosecution
prosecutor
sect
sectarian
sequel
sequence
sequential

A list of words to print out for students can be found on the Digital Resource CD (filename: wordlists.pdf).

Teacher Background Information and Tips

Base *sequ-, secut-* = "follow"

The Latin base *sequ-, secut-,* which means "follow," appears in many words from social studies. Such words as *persecution, prosecution, executive, execution, sects,* and *sectarian* are all built on these bases. Some words refer to the act of "following" laws and legal procedures; others refer to people who "follow" cult leaders of "sects."

These bases attach to many Latin directional prefixes. Although these terms can be challenging for students, the essential meaning of the words can be understood by examining the prefix and base.

For a glossary of words with these roots, see the Digital Resource CD (filename: rootsglossary.pdf).

Name: _____ Date: _____

About the Root:
Who/What Will You Follow?

Directions: Read the information. Then answer the questions.

The Latin base *sequ-, secut-* means "follow." It appears in many words from social studies. Such words as *persecution, prosecution, sects,* and *sectarian* are all built on these bases. Because the ancient Romans were experts at producing laws, many words from this Latin base refer to "following" laws and legal procedures. Other words refer to people who "follow" leaders of "sects."

Even the words *execute, execution,* and *executive* are "following" words. Because these words begin with the prefix *ex-* (meaning "out"), which ends in the consonant *x*, we drop the *s* from the base. The letter *x* has a built-in *s* sound!

Talk with a partner to answer these questions. Write your responses.

◎ How does the word *sequel* mean "follow"?

_____

_____

_____

_____

◎ How does the word *sect* mean follow?

_____

_____

_____

_____

Name: _____   Date: _____

About the Root: Civics:
An Execution Sentence

Directions: Read the information. Then answer the questions.

Have you ever thought about why the word *execute* can mean "put to death at the hands of the state"? In some states, convicted criminals may receive a death sentence. The judge orders death at a set day and time. The *executioner* is the officer responsible for "following out," or *executing*, the order. This is called *capital punishment*. But our language refers to this as *execution* and not as *killing*. Because such words as *kill* and *death* make us feel uncomfortable, we use the legal-sounding word—*execution*—to calm our uneasiness. *Execute* is a euphemism (meaning a substitution of a mild word for a harsh one) for "put to death." People opposed to capital punishment try to expose this euphemism by calling it "state-sanctioned killing."

◎ What is your belief about *execution* as a form of punishment? Why?

_____

_____

_____

_____

◎ A state governor has the authority to issue a *stay of execution* before a convicted criminal is to be put to death. What do you think the phrase *stay of execution* means?

_____

_____

_____

_____

_____

_____

_____

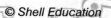

Name: _____ Date: _____

About the Root: World History:
Persecution

. . . .

Directions: Read the information. Then answer the question.

Unfortunately, people have mistreated one another throughout history. Sometimes, people are singled out for *persecution*. Reasons include religious beliefs, the color of someone's skin, a person's nationality, or even gender. The Latin prefix *per-*, which means "through," also means "wrongly." So, the word *persecution* means that victims are "wrongly followed." They are subjected to violence and injustice. Here are some examples of this kind of cruelty:

◎ Romans persecuted early Christians

◎ The Nazis persecuted Jews

◎ European settlers persecuted Native Americans

Select one example of persecution. How were the persecuted people subjected to violence and injustice?

_____

_____

_____

_____

Name: _____   Date: _____

Divide and Conquer:
Follow the Leader

Directions: Use the Base/Prefix Bank to help you identify the roots of the words below. *X* means the word does not contain that element. Write the letter from the Definition Bank for the correct word.

Base/Prefix Bank

ex- = "out"   *per-* = "through," "wrongly"   *pro-* = "forward," "ahead"

Definition Bank

A. a group of people who break away from the main group to follow another leader or belief

B. to pursue a criminal suspect

C. to carry out a plan or order and implement it

D. one who holds a high position of administrative authority

E. mistreatment of others, usually based on prejudice or bigotry

Word	First Base/ Prefix Means	Second Base/ Suffix Means	Definition
1. persecution			
2. executive			
3. prosecute			
4. sect		X	
5. execute			

Name: _____ Date: _____

Making Connections:
Making Meaning

Directions: Using the word *follow*, explain what these phrases and sentences mean.

1. A large sign in a drugstore reads, *Shoplifters Will Be Prosecuted*.

_____
_____
_____

2. The Pilgrims who came to America were fleeing *religious persecution*.

_____
_____
_____
_____

3. *Sectarian violence* broke out once again in the politically unstable region.

_____
_____
_____

4. The state governor surprised everyone when he issued a *stay of execution* for the convicted criminal.

_____
_____
_____

5. Trace the *sequence of events* leading up to the crisis.

_____
_____
_____

Base equ(i)-, egal-

equ(i)-, egal- = "equal," "fair"

Standards

Uses common, grade-appropriate Greek or Latin affixes and roots as clues to the meaning of a word

Determines the meaning of words and phrases as they are used in a text, including vocabulary specific to domains related to history/social studies

By the end of the year, reads and comprehends literary nonfiction in the grades 6–8 text complexity band proficiently, with scaffolding as needed at the high end of the range

Materials

- *About the Root: Government: The Scales of Justice* (page 86)

- *About the Root: World History: Egalitarianism* and *Geography: The Great Circle of the Earth* (page 87)

- *Divide and Conquer: Fairness and Equality* (page 88)

- *Making Connections: Complete the Sentence* (page 89)

Teacher Preparation

- Read and review the background information about the base *equ(i)-, egal-* on page 85 to familiarize yourself with their context in social studies and government.

- Read and review the glossary of the base found on the Digital Resource CD (filename: rootsglossary.pdf) for additional support.

Guided Practice

About the Root

1. Distribute copies of pages 86 and 87 to students. Ask pairs of students to think about words they already know with these bases. Provide time for discussion after pairs have brainstormed a list.

2. Have students read the passages and answer the questions. Students can work independently or with partners. You may want to conclude with a whole-class discussion to review students' answers and reinforce the meaning of the roots in context.

Divide and Conquer

3. Distribute copies of *Divide and Conquer* (page 88). As you guide students through the activity page, use questions like these to generate discussion about each of the words:

   - Where is the meaning of "equal" or "fair" in the word _____?

   - Where might you see the word _____?

   - Can you think of an example of _____?

Base equ(i)-, egal- (cont.)

Making Connections

4. Distribute copies of *Making Connections* (page 89).

5. Have students preview all of the sentences before completing the activity sheet.

6. Conclude with a whole-class discussion that focuses on root meaning. You may also wish to invite partners to rewrite a few of the sentences, maintaining meaning but not using the words that were written in the blanks.

Words with equ(i)-, egal-

adequate
Ecuador
egalitarian
egalitarianism
equable
equal
equality
equator
equatorial
equidistant
equilateral
equilibrium
equinox
equitable
equity
equivocal
equivocate
inadequate
inequity
unequivocal

A list of words to print out for students can be found on the Digital Resource CD (filename: wordlists.pdf).

Teacher Background Information and Tips

Base equ(i)-, egal- = "equal," "fair"

The Latin base *equ(i)-, egal-*, which means "equal," "fair," appears in many words from social studies. The dual meanings of the base "equal" and "fair" are connected. When things are equally divided or apportioned, everyone receives a fair share. The word *equality* connotes impartiality and balance as opposed to favoring one side over another. The base appears in many important phrases from American and world history, for example, *equality* before the law; *Equal* Rights Amendment; separate but *equal*; social *inequality*; the *equity* of justice; social *inequities*; and *egalitarianism*.

This base also appears in words from world geography referring to the *equator*, *equatorial* climates, and the South American country of *Ecuador*, through which the *equator* passes.

Important social studies words that are built on this base include *equal, inequity, equanimity, equator,* and *equivocate*.

For a glossary of words with this root, see the Digital Resource CD (filename: rootsglossary.pdf).

Name: _____ Date: _____

About the Root: Government:
The Scales of Justice

- -

Directions: Read the information. Then answer the questions.

> The Latin base *equ(i)-, egal-* means "equal," "fair." It appears in many words in social studies and other content areas. The dual meanings of the base "equal" and "fair" are connected. When things are equally divided, everyone receives a fair share. Explain how the meaning of the following phrases includes ideas about "equal" or "fair":

◎ "All men are created *equal...*"

_____

_____

◎ *Equality* before the law

_____

_____

◎ The base also appears in words from world geography referring to the *equator.* How does *equator* mean "equal"?

_____

_____

> Have you ever wondered why statues of Justice depict a blindfolded woman holding a pair of scales in her raised hands? In order to make the pans of the scale balance, the weights on each side must be *equal*. Only when things are *equal* are they fair. Wearing a blindfold, Lady Justice does not look at the people making their cases before her. She does not want to unfairly favor one person over another just because of the way they look. This is why we say that courts "hear" (rather than "see" or "view") a case. The justice system believes in *equity* before the law, ever striving to treat with fairness "all men [who] are created equal."

◎ Have you ever heard the expression "justice is blind"? What do you think it means? Write your thoughts on a separate sheet of paper.

Name: _____ Date: _____

About the Root: World History:
Egalitarianism

. . . .

Directions: Read the passages. Then answer the questions.

Egalitarians believe in *equal rights* for all people. They believe that all people should be treated the same. They also believe that all people should have the same opportunities. Belief in the *equality* of all humanity is one of the marks of an advanced civilization. The word *egalitarian* is spelled with a *g* instead of with a *qu* because it comes from the French word *égalité*. This word means "equality." The motto of the French Revolution of 1789 was "Liberté, Égalité, Fraternité."

◎ Can you guess what these three French words (*liberté, égalité, fraternité*) mean?

_____

_____

◎ Do you consider yourself an *egalitarian*? Why or why not?

_____

_____

_____

Geography: The Great Circle of the Earth

Shaped like a huge globe or sphere, Earth is broadest at the *equator*, which we call "the great circle of the earth." Answer the questions below on a separate sheet of paper.

◎ Why do you think we call this geographical dividing line the *equator*?

◎ Do you know what we call the northern half and the southern half of the earth? (**Hint:** The Greek prefix *hemi-* means "half.")

Name: _____ Date: _____

Divide and Conquer:
Fairness and Equality

Directions: Use the Base/Prefix Bank to help you identify the roots of the words below. Write the letter from the Definition Bank for the correct word.

Base/Prefix Bank

ad- = "to," "toward," "add to" *in-* = "not" *voc-* = "voice," "speak"

Definition Bank

A. unfairness; social imbalance

B. philosophy promoting the equality of all human beings

C. to employ vague and misleading language that does not commit to one side or position

D. barely acceptable; meeting minimum standards

E. pertaining to or located on the equator

Word	First Base/ Prefix Means	Second Base/ Suffix Means	Definition
1. egalitarianism		*-itarianism* = belief in	
2. equivocate			
3. adequate			
4. inequity			
5. equatorial		*-(at)orial* = pertaining to	

Name: _____ Date: _____

Making Connections:
Complete the Sentence

Directions: Use the words from the Word Bank to complete the sentences below.

Word Bank

egalitarian   equitable   inadequate
equator   equivocated   inequity

1. The South American country of Ecuador received its name because the _____ cuts through it.

2. Most people who campaign for human rights around the world share _____ views.

3. Afraid he might offend some members of the audience, the candidate _____ in his response to a question on global warming.

4. It would be a great _____ if the defendant were found guilty simply because he could not afford a good lawyer.

5. The voters found the candidate's responses _____ and quickly withdrew their support.

6. I am sure that we can arrive at an _____ solution.

You Try It!

Use two of the following words in sentences: *equatorial, equivocal, equality.* Leave a blank for the word. Then share your sentences with a partner. Ask him or her to fill in the blanks.

_____

_____

_____

Bases *greg-* and *integr-*

greg- = "flock," "herd"
integr- = "whole"

Standards

Uses common, grade-appropriate Greek or Latin affixes and roots as clues to the meaning of a word

Determines the meaning of words and phrases as they are used in a text, including vocabulary specific to domains related to history/social studies

By the end of the year, reads and comprehends literary nonfiction in the grades 6–8 text complexity band proficiently, with scaffolding as needed at the high end of the range

Materials

- *About the Root: American History: A Whole Society* (page 93)

- *About the Root: Culture and Society: Returning Soldiers* (page 94)

- *About the Root: Racial Segregation* (page 95)

- *Divide and Conquer: Together and Apart* (page 96)

- *Making Connections: Who/What Am I?* (page 97)

Teacher Preparation

- Read and review the background information about the bases *greg-* and *integr-* on page 92 to familiarize yourself with their context in social studies.

- Read and review the glossary of the bases found on the Digital Resource CD (filename: rootsglossary.pdf) for additional support.

Guided Practice

About the Root

1. Distribute copies of pages 93, 94, and/or 95 to students. Ask partners to think about words they already know with these bases. Invite sharing.

2. Have students read the remaining passages and answer the questions. Students can work independently or with partners. You may want to conclude with a whole-class discussion to review students' answers and reinforce the meaning of the roots in context.

Divide and Conquer

3. Distribute copies of *Divide and Conquer* (page 96). As you guide students through the activity page, use questions like these to generate discussion about each of the words:

   - Where is the meaning of "flock," "herd" or "whole" in the word _____?

   - Where might you see the word _____?

   - Can you think of an example of _____?

Bases greg- and integr- (cont.)

Making Connections

4. Distribute copies of *Making Connections* (page 97).

5. Have students read all of the definitions before completing the activity sheet.

6. Conclude with a whole-class discussion that focuses on root meaning.

Words with greg- and integr-

aggregate
congregate
congregation
desegregate
desegregation
disintegrate
disintegration
egregious
gregarious
integer
integral
integrate
integration
integrity
reintegrate
reintegration
segregate
segregation

A list of words to print out for students can be found on the Digital Resource CD (filename: wordlists.pdf).

Teacher Background Information and Tips

Bases *greg-* = "flock," "herd" and *integr-* = "whole"

The Latin base *greg-* means "flock," "herd" and the Latin base *integr-* means "whole." These two bases appear in social studies words describing communities of people (as in *congregate* or *congregations*) and race relations in American history (*segregation, desegregation,* and *integration*). These two bases provide powerful metaphors for *integrated communities* that are "whole" and for *segregated societies* that are divided into separate groups.

The base *greg-*, with its metaphor of "flock," can connote religious communities. A *congregation* "flocks together" in worship (Latin prefix *con-* = "with," "together"), following a leader who in some traditions is called a *pastor* (a Latin word meaning "shepherd"). The metaphor of the pastor and his or her flock is especially pronounced in the American Civil Rights movement, in which the Reverend Dr. Martin Luther King Jr. strove to end racial *segregation*. The "flock," "herd" metaphor is striking as one considers this movement. *Congregations* often provided the organizational structure for campaigning to end *segregation* (the setting "apart" or "aside" of "flocks" of people into separate groupings; Latin prefix *se-* = "aside," "apart").

The Latin base *integr-* has a literal and metaphorical meaning of "whole." Most students will be familiar with the mathematical term *integer*, a "whole" number. When something *disintegrates*, it crumbles, falling "apart" (Latin prefix *dis-* = "apart," "in different directions") from an originally "whole" state or condition. Similarly, *integrity* is "wholeness" of character. *Integrated* societies are "whole" in the sense that they are not broken up into disconnected groups. On their return to civilian life, soldiers must be *reintegrated* into a civilian society.

Important social studies words that are built on these bases include *gregarious, congregate, aggregate, desegregate,* and *reintegrate.*

For a glossary of words with these roots, see the Digital Resource CD (filename: rootsglossary.pdf).

Name: _____ Date: _____

About the Root: American History:
A Whole Society

. . . .

Directions: Read the information. Then answer the questions.

> The Latin base *greg-* means "flock," "herd." The Latin base *integr-* means "whole." These two bases appear in social studies words describing communities of people (as in *congregate* or *congregations*). The bases are also in words that describe race relations in American history (e.g., *segregation, desegregation,* and *integration*). These two bases provide powerful metaphors for *integrated communities* that are "whole" and for *segregated societies* that are divided into separate groups.

◎ Describe an integrated community.

_____

_____

_____

◎ Describe a segregated community.

_____

_____

_____

> On August 28, 1963, the Reverend Dr. Martin Luther King Jr. delivered a famous speech. He spoke to more than 200,000 people at the Lincoln Memorial in Washington, DC. He wanted to end racial *segregation*, still practiced in the United States. He hoped for a racially *integrated* society. He said, "I have a dream that my four little children will one day live in a nation where they will not be judged by the color of their skin but by the content of their character."
>
>
>
> Think about these words. While talking about racial *integration*, Dr. King spoke of "content of character." This is another way of saying *integrity*. Both the words *integration* and *integrity* have a base meaning of "whole."

◎ We say that a person of good character has *integrity*. In what ways does an *integrated* society have *integrity*? Explain your thinking on a separate sheet of paper.

Name: _____   Date: _____

About the Root: Culture and Society:
Returning Soldiers

Directions: Read the information. Then answer the question.

When soldiers go away to war, their friends and family often worry about them. Everyone is relieved when a soldier returns home safely. But the soldier may still have problems to solve. *Reintegration* into society can be a challenge.

Soldiers are often proud of their service to our country. They want to return to family, friends, and work. But they may have medical or psychological problems to solve. They may even have legal or financial problems. Then there is the challenge of stepping back into civilian society. All of this can be stressful. Government, religious, and community agencies try to help ex-soldiers *reintegrate.*

◎ How might a community agency help returning soldiers *reintegrate* into society?

_____

_____

_____

_____

_____

_____

◎ Why might soldiers have difficulty reintegrating into their communities?

_____

_____

_____

Name: _____ Date: _____

About the Root:
Racial Segregation

Directions: Read the information. Then answer the question.

We all know that racial *segregation* is outlawed in the United States—and for good reason. When a society segregates people according to their race, an injustice is committed against them. The Declaration of Independence states that "all men are created equal, that they are endowed by their Creator with certain unalienable rights, that among these are life, liberty, and the pursuit of happiness."

But a racially segregated society treats citizens with inequality. In a segregated society, some people are denied basic human rights, such as the right to equal opportunities in housing, employment, or education. Long ago, some people were even denied the right to sit at a table in the same restaurant with others of a different race! Racially segregated societies do not provide equal access to liberty and the pursuit of happiness.

Far from honoring the dignity of each and every human being, segregation clusters people into "herds." This is what the Latin base *greg-* means. In segregation, people are "herded" into separate clusters and kept apart from one another. A segregated society can never be an equal society. This is why federal United States law mandates racial desegregation.

◎ Talk to a partner. Do you agree that a "segregated society can never be an equal society"? Why?

_____

_____

_____

_____

_____

_____

Name: _____ Date: _____

Divide and Conquer:
Together and Apart

Directions: Use the Base/Prefix Bank to help you identify the roots of the words below. Write the letter from the Definition Bank for the correct word.

Base/Prefix Bank

con- = "with," "together"

dis- = "apart," "in different directions," "not"

re- = "back," "again"

se- = "apart," "aside"

Definition Bank

A. to flock together; to meet for worship or prayer

B. to put back into the whole unit or community; to restore to society at large

C. wholeness of character; trustworthiness; honesty and honorability

D. to fall apart or crumble

E. to divide and separate into groups

Word	First Base/ Prefix Means	Second Base/ Suffix Means	Definition
1. disintegrate			
2. congregate			
3. segregate			
4. reintegrate			
5. integrity		*-ity* = state of, quality of	

Name: _____ Date: _____

Making Connections:
Who/What Am I?

. . . .

Directions: Match each word in the first column with its speaker in the second column.

Word	Speaker
_____ **1.** integer	**A.** I am the inclusion of everyone to create a whole society.
_____ **2.** disintegration	**B** I am a whole number, not a fraction.
_____ **3.** congregation	**C.** I am a total collapse and falling apart.
_____ **4.** segregation	**D.** I am a party animal! I am often the most sociable person in my group.
_____ **5.** integration	**E.** I am the division of a society along racial lines.
_____ **6.** gregarious	**F.** We are a worshipping community.
_____ **7.** aggregate	**G.** I am the sum total of many numbers added together.

You Try It!

Use two of the words *integral, egregious,* or *aggregate* in a sentence.

_____

_____

_____

_____

_____

_____

Bases *the(o)-* and *de(i)-, divin-*

the(o)-, de(i)-, divin- = "god"

Standards

Uses common, grade-appropriate Greek or Latin affixes and roots as clues to the meaning of a word

Determines the meaning of words and phrases as they are used in a text, including vocabulary specific to domains related to history/social studies

By the end of the year, reads and comprehends literary nonfiction in the grades 6–8 text complexity band proficiently, with scaffolding as needed at the high end of the range

Materials

- *About the Root: Culture and Society: Belief in One God or Many Gods* (page 101)

- *About the Root: World History: The Deification of Public Figures?* (page 102)

- *About the Root: Atheists and Agnostics* (page 103)

- *Divide and Conquer: One or Many?* (page 104)

- *Making Connections: Who/What Are We?* (page 105)

Teacher Preparation

- Read and review the background information about the bases *the(o)-* and *de(i)-, divin-* on page 100 to familiarize yourself with their context in history, culture, and society.

- Read and review the glossary of the bases found on the Digital Resource CD (filename: rootsglossary.pdf) for additional support.

Guided Practice

About the Root

1. Distribute copies of pages 101, 102, and/or 103 to students. Ask partners to think about words they already know with these bases. Invite sharing.

2. Have students read the passages and answer the questions. Students can work independently or with partners. You may want to conclude with a whole-class discussion to review students' answers and reinforce the meaning of the roots in context.

Divide and Conquer

3. Distribute copies of *Divide and Conquer* (page 104). As you guide students through the activity page, use questions like these to generate discussion about each of the words:

   - Where is the meaning of "god" in the word _____?

   - Where might you see the word _____?

   - Can you think of an example of _____?

Bases *the(o)-* and *de(i)-*, *divin-* (cont.)

Making Connections

4. Distribute copies of *Making Connections* (page 105).

5. Have students read all of the definitions before completing the activity sheet.

6. Conclude with a whole-class discussion that focuses on root meaning.

Words with *de(i)-*, *divin-*, *the(o)-*

apostheosis	monotheistic
atheism	pantheon
atheist	Pantheon
atheistic	polytheism
deification	polytheist
deify	polytheistic
deism	theism
deity	theocracy
divine	theocratic
divinity	theologian
monotheism	theological
monotheist	theology

A list of words to print out for students can be found on the Digital Resource CD (filename: wordlists.pdf).

Spelling Hints:

It is conventional to spell *God* with an uppercase *g* when referring to monotheistic religions because *God* is a proper name. When referring to polytheistic traditions, however, which recognize many gods, the words *god* and *god*s are written with a lowercase *g*. For example, in ancient Greek polytheism, the 12 *gods* (lowercase *g*) of Mount Olympus had such names as Zeus, Athena, Apollo, and Aphrodite (capitalized proper names).

Teacher Background Information and Tips

Bases *the(o)-* and *de(i)-*, divin- = "god"

The Greek and Latin bases meaning "god" (Greek *the(o)-*; Latin *de(i)-*, *divin-*) appear in many social studies words related to world cultures and beliefs. The Greek base is found in technical words describing religion as an intellectual or spiritual discipline (*theology, theism*) and as a variety of belief systems practiced by different cultures and societies (*monotheism, polytheism, theocracy, apotheosis*). The Latin base occurs in more general-usage words describing aspects of and attitudes toward God or gods (*divine, divinity, deity*). Important social studies words that are built on these bases include *theology, monotheism, atheism, deity,* and *divinity*.

For a glossary of words with these roots, see the Digital Resource CD (filename: rootsglossary.pdf).

Name: _____ Date: _____

About the Root: Culture and Society:
Belief in One God or Many Gods

Directions: Read the information. Then answer the questions.

The Greek and Latin bases meaning "god" (Greek *the(o)-* and Latin *de(i)-* and *divin-)* appear in many social studies words about world cultures and beliefs. The Greek base is found in more technical words. The Latin base occurs in more general-usage words describing aspects of and attitudes toward God or gods.

Words about religion can be long and technical. Luckily, Greek-based words built on *the-* are easy to figure out. This base attaches to many Greek prefixes and suffixes. Two common suffixes for *the-* words are *-ism*, meaning "belief in," and *-ist*, meaning "one who believes in."

See if you can figure out what these paired words mean:

◎ *monotheism/monotheist*

_____

_____

◎ *polytheism/polytheist*

_____

_____

Name: _____ Date: _____

About the Root: World History:
The Deification of Public Figures?

Directions: Read the information. Then answer the question.

Ancient Romans believed that their dead emperors became gods. As gods, the emperors lived on Mount Olympus and protected Rome. But even a Roman Emperor could have a sense of humor about the absurd notion of turning into a god. On his deathbed in 79 A.D., the Emperor Vespasian did not say, "I am dying." He said, "Why, I think I'm becoming a god!" The Roman Senate *deified* him immediately, of course!

Washington, DC, is full of monuments to our past leaders. The Lincoln Memorial displays a huge statue of President Abraham Lincoln seated inside a Greek temple with 36 columns, one for each state of the Union at the time of his death. The Jefferson Memorial, housing a tall statue of Thomas Jefferson, is modeled after the Roman Pantheon, a temple dedicated to "all the gods." These statues and monuments remind us that these leaders and their achievements were important. But if an ancient Roman were to view them, he would say, "Why, I think I am looking at a god!"

IN THIS TEMPLE
AS IN THE HEARTS OF THE PEOPLE
FOR WHOM HE SAVED THE UNION
THE MEMORY OF ABRAHAM LINCOLN
IS ENSHRINED FOREVER

Today, we do not believe that a person can become a god. But whenever we put a person on a pedestal and elevate them in our eyes, we say that we *deify* them.

◎ Think of another famous person who has been *deified* because of his or her achievements and explain why you believe he or she has been *deified*.

_____

_____

_____

_____

_____

Name: _____   Date: _____

About the Root:
Atheists and Agnostics

Directions: Read the information. Then answer the question.

Some people confuse the words *agnostic* and *atheist*. But if you divide and conquer the words, you can quickly see how they differ. Both words begin with the Greek prefix *a-,* which means "not," "without." So, an *atheist* believes that there is "no" "God." But the word *agnostic* is built on a different base. The Greek *gnos-* means "know," "knowledge." An *agnostic* might say, "I do not know whether God exists." An *atheist* expresses a stronger opinion, firmly maintaining that there is no God.

An ancient Greek philosopher named Protagoras wrote, "As for the gods, I have no way of knowing whether they exist or not, nor what they look like. For the topic is difficult and human life is short."

◎ Was Protagoras an *atheist* or an *agnostic*? How can you tell?

_____

_____

_____

_____

_____

_____

_____

Name: _____ Date: _____

Divide and Conquer:
One or Many?

Directions: Use the Base/Prefix Bank to help you identify the roots of the words below. Write the letter from the Definition Bank for the correct word.

Base/Prefix Bank

mono- = "only one," "single"   *pan-* = "all"   *poly-* = "many"

Definition Bank

A. gods

B. all the gods acknowledged in a polytheistic system

C. worshipping only one god or deity

D. to glorify another as if he or she were a god

E. belief in many gods

Word	First Base/ Prefix Means	Second Base/ Suffix Means	Definition
1. polytheism			
2. deities		X	
3. monotheistic			
4. pantheon			
5. deify		*-(i)fy* = make	

Name: _____ Date: _____

Making Connections:
Who/What Are We?

Directions: Match each word or phrase in the first column with its speaker in the second column.

Word/Phrase	Speaker
_____ **1.** monotheistic religions	**A.** We declare that God does not exist.
_____ **2.** deists	**B.** We recognize one, and only one, God.
_____ **3.** pantheon	**C.** We are all the gods named in a multigod faith.
_____ **4.** atheists	**D.** We maintain that God can be comprehended by reason alone. We do not need organized religion to reveal truths to us.
_____ **5.** polytheistic religions	**E.** We acknowledge many different gods in our faith system.
_____ **6.** theological disputes	**F.** We are disagreements over the nature of God and religion.
_____ **7.** divinity schools	**G.** We are colleges and universities specializing in religious studies.

You Try It!

Use two of these words *divine, divinity, theological,* or *deification* in your own sentence(s):

_____

_____

_____

_____

Base vert-, vers-

vert-, vers- = "turn," "change"

Standards

Uses common, grade-appropriate Greek or Latin affixes and roots as clues to the meaning of a word

Determines the meaning of words and phrases as they are used in a text, including vocabulary specific to domains related to history/social studies

By the end of the year, reads and comprehends literary nonfiction in the grades 6–8 text complexity band proficiently, with scaffolding as needed at the high end of the range

Materials

- *About the Root: World History: The World, So Diverse, Is One* (page 109)

- *About the Root: The Turning of Time* (page 110)

- *About the Root: American History: The Conversion of the Native Americans* (page 111)

- *Divide and Conquer: Many Changes* (page 112)

- *Making Connections: Fill in the Blank* (page 113)

Teacher Preparation

- Read and review the background information about the base *vert-*, *vers-* on page 108 to familiarize yourself with their context in history and social studies.

- Read and review the glossary of the base found on the Digital Resource CD (filename: rootsglossary.pdf) for additional support.

Guided Practice

About the Root

1. Distribute copies of pages 109, 110, and/or 111 to students. If necessary, remind students about literal (actual) and figurative (symbolic or abstract) meanings. You could use these sentences as examples:

   - I *see* your point.

   - I *see* the school bus coming.

2. Have students read the passages and answer the questions. Students can work independently or with partners. You may want to conclude with a whole-class discussion to review students' answers and reinforce the meaning of the roots in context.

Base vert-, vers- *(cont.)*

Divide and Conquer

3. Distribute copies of *Divide and Conquer* (page 112). As you guide students through the activity page, use questions like these to generate discussion about each of the words:

• Where is the meaning of "turn" or "change" in the word _____?

• Where might you see the word _____?

• Can you think of an example of _____?

Making Connections

4. Distribute copies of *Making Connections* (page 113).

5. Have students preview all of the sentences before completing the activity sheet.

6. Conclude with a whole-class discussion that focuses on root meaning. You may also ask pairs of students to rewrite a couple of sentences to maintain meaning without using the words put in the blanks. You can then invite sharing and talk with students about the process of rewriting.

Words with vert-, vers-

adverse	extrovert
adversity	extroverted
advertise	inadvertent
advertisement	incontrovertible
anniversary	introvert
averse	introverted
aversion	invert
avert	inverse
controversial	inversion
controversy	pervert
conversion	revert
convert	subvert
convertible	traverse
diverse	universal
diversion	universe
diversity	versatile
divert	version
	vertigo

A list of words to print out for students can be found on the Digital Resource CD (filename: wordlists.pdf).

Teacher Background Information and Tips

Base *vert-, vers-* = "turn," "change"

The Latin base *vert-, vers-,* meaning "turn," "change," generates a large number of English words, many of which are related to social studies and other content areas. Students may already know some derivatives but may not have associated them with the base meaning of "turn" or "change." Words like *convert, universe, diversity, controversy, advertise, subvert, version,* and *vertical* are all built on this base. The base attaches to no fewer than 14 Latin prefixes.

This lesson presents derivatives that students are likely to encounter in social studies texts dealing with world cultures (e.g., *universe, diversity, conversion*) and history (e.g., *controversy, subvert, subversive, avert, adverse, adversity*).

Important social studies words that are built on this base include *diverse, cultural diversity, anniversary, divert,* and *perverse.*

For a glossary of words with this root, see the Digital Resource CD (filename: rootsglossary.pdf).

Name: _____ Date: _____

About the Root: World History:
The World, So Diverse, Is One

Directions: Read the information. Then answer the questions.

> The Latin base *vert-, vers-* means "turn," "change." Many words contain this base, including social studies words. Sometimes, the idea of "turning" is literal in *vert-, vers-* words. Other times, the "turning" is figurative.

◎ Is the "turning" in *reverse* literal or figurative? How do you know?

_____

_____

_____

◎ Is the "turning" in *convert* literal or figurative? How do you know?

_____

_____

_____

> The Romans gave us the word and the concept of *diversity*. As they expanded their empire, they came into contact with many different peoples. They saw people who lived around the Mediterranean Sea, including Egypt and Libya. They also saw other Europeans and Asians. These people spoke different languages, worshipped different gods, and observed different customs. The Romans brought these diverse populations into their empire and made them Roman subjects. Yet they allowed them to maintain their own ways of life, speak their own languages, and keep their own customs. Many of the new subjects had to pay taxes to Rome and recognize the emperor's authority. It is hardly a wonder that *diversity* is a Latin-based word.
>
> But as Roman philosophers thought about this *diverse* world, they searched to find what everyone had in common. They sought to understand the *universal* things that all human beings share. In the third century A.D., a scholar named Lucius Ampelius came up with this explanation of the word for *world*: "The world, in which all things exist, is the *universality* and sum total of everything." The one *universe*, it seems, is full of differences!

◎ What do you think the Romans understood about the value of diversity? Write your thoughts on a separate sheet of paper.

Name: _____   Date: _____

About the Root:
The Turning of Time

Directions: Read the information. Then answer the question.

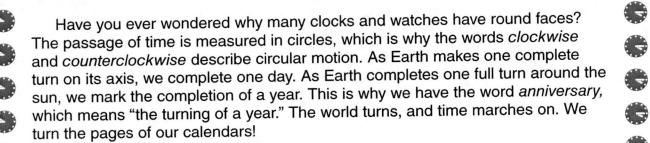

Have you ever wondered why many clocks and watches have round faces? The passage of time is measured in circles, which is why the words *clockwise* and *counterclockwise* describe circular motion. As Earth makes one complete turn on its axis, we complete one day. As Earth completes one full turn around the sun, we mark the completion of a year. This is why we have the word *anniversary,* which means "the turning of a year." The world turns, and time marches on. We turn the pages of our calendars!

◎ Using the word *turn*, explain what we do when we *reverse* the movement of the hands of a clock or watch.

_____

_____

_____

Name: _____ Date: _____

About the Root: American History:
The Conversion of the Native Americans

Directions: Read the information. Then answer the questions.

Historians believe that more than 500 different Native American tribes lived in the New World at the time of Christopher Columbus. These people had their own languages, religions, and ways of life. Little is known for certain about their various religions because Native Americans did not write. Moreover, the settlers who wrote about Native Americans were probably influenced by their own assumptions and prejudices. Their opinions may not have been accurate.

Many European settlers believed the Native Americans were "heathens." They wanted to *convert* them to Christianity. In fact, a priest was charged with this very task was on Columbus's second voyage. This man, along with many other Spanish and later French explorers, tried to *convert* the native peoples.

◎ Explain the meaning of the word *convert* using the concept of turning or changing.

_____

_____

_____

_____

◎ Do you think people should try to *convert* others to their religions? Why or why not?

_____

_____

_____

_____

Name: _____ Date: _____

Divide and Conquer:
Many Changes

. . . .

Directions: Use the Base/Prefix Bank to help you identify the roots of the words below. Write the letter from the Definition Bank for the correct word.

Base/Prefix Bank

con- = "with," "together"

di- = "apart," "in different directions"

contro- = "against"

sub- = "under," "below," "up from under"

uni- = "one"

Definition Bank

A. encompassing all people and things; whole and entire

B. varied; made up of many different things or people

C. to undermine and attempt to overthrow

D. the adoption of a different religion or belief

E. characterized by disagreement and disputes

Word	First Base/ Prefix Means	Second Base/ Suffix Means	Definition
1. diverse			
2. controversial			
3. universal			
4. conversion			
5. subvert			

Name: _____ Date: _____

Making Connections:
Fill in the Blank

· ·

Directions: Use the words from the Word Bank to complete the sentences.

Word Bank

| avert | controversial | convert | subversives | version |

1. North American history contains many accounts of Spanish missionaries who attempted to _____ Native Americans to Christianity.

2. As soon as the dictator seized power, he rounded up all of the political _____ and had them executed.

3. Government leaders and economists held a conference in hopes that they could _____ a global financial disaster.

4. The King James _____ of the Bible has had a profound impact on the English language.

5. When addressing large audiences, a speaker should avoid _____ subjects that might offend listeners.

You Try It!

Use one or more of the following words in your own sentence: *universal, versatile, diversity*. Leave a blank where the word belongs. Then share your sentence with a partner. Ask him or her to fill in the blank.

_____

_____

_____

_____

Bases *human-* and *anthrop(o)-*

human-, anthrop(o)- = "mankind," "human being"

Standards

Uses common, grade-appropriate Greek or Latin affixes and roots as clues to the meaning of a word

Determines the meaning of words and phrases as they are used in a text, including vocabulary specific to domains related to history/social studies

By the end of the year, reads and comprehends literary nonfiction in the grades 6–8 text complexity band proficiently, with scaffolding as needed at the high end of the range

Materials

- *About the Root: World History: The Rise of Humanism and the Humanities* (page 117)

- *About the Root: A Double Entendre: Habitat for Humanity* (page 118)

- *About the Root: World History: The Anthropomorphic Gods of Greece* (page 119)

- *Divide and Conquer: Being Human* (page 120)

- *Making Connections: Who/What Am I?* (page 121)

Teacher Preparation

- Read and review the background information about the bases *human-* and *anthrop(o)-* on page 116 to familiarize yourself with their context in history and social studies.

- Read and review the glossary of the bases found on the Digital Resource CD (filename: rootsglossary.pdf) for additional support.

Guided Practice

About the Root

1. Distribute copies of pages 117, 118, and/or 119 to students. Write *human-* and *anthrop(o)-* on the board and explain their meanings ("human being," "mankind"). Ask pairs of students to think about words they already know with these bases. Invite sharing.

2. Have students read the passages and answer the questions. Students can work independently or with partners. You may want to conclude with a whole-class discussion to review students' answers and reinforce the meaning of the roots in context.

Divide and Conquer

3. Distribute copies of *Divide and Conquer* (page 120). As you guide students through the activity page, use questions like these to generate discussion about each of the words:

   - Where is the meaning of "mankind" or "human being" in the word _____?

   - Where might you see the word _____?

   - Can you think of an example of _____?

Bases *human-* and *anthrop(o)-* *(cont.)*

Making Connections

4. Distribute copies of *Making Connections* (page 121).

5. Have students read all of the definitions before completing the activity sheet.

6. Conclude with a whole-class discussion that focuses on root meaning.

Words with *anthrop(o)-*, *human-*

anthropocentric	humanity
anthropoid	inhuman
anthropologist	inhumane
anthropology	misanthrope
anthropomorphic	misanthropic
human	philanthropic
humane	philanthropist
humanist	philanthropy
humanistic	subhuman
humanities	superhuman

A list of words to print out for students can be found on the Digital Resource CD (filename: wordlists.pdf).

Spelling Hints:

Words beginning with the Greek base *anthrop(o)-* tend to be long but can be easily "divided and conquered" at the point of the connecting *o*, which joins Greek bases. Most social studies words based on Latin *human-* do not include prefixes (except for *sub-*, *super-,* and negative *in-*).

Teacher Background Information and Tips

Bases *human-* and *anthrop(o)-* = "mankind," "human being"

The Latin base *human-* and the Greek base *anthrop(o)-* mean "mankind," "human being." These roots appear in many words from social studies. Words built on the Latin base refer to human beings and the qualities of being human, as opposed to animals not endowed with speech or the capacity for developed rational thought. Examples of *human-* words include *humanity, humanitarian, humanist, humane,* and *inhumane.*

An interesting distinction marks the adjectives *human* and *humane.* The word *human* refers to the simpler, weaker, and often flawed aspects of our nature, as in the sayings "to err is *human*," "he's only *human*," and "*human* error." The phrase "*human* kindness" connotes our simple and innate instincts. But the adjective *humane* refers to our nobler and more civilized instincts and tendencies, as in "a *humane* gesture," "the *humane* thing to do," and "The *Humane* Society." The noun *humanity* embraces the concepts of both *human* and *humane. Humanity* consists of all mankind, but when we "show our *humanity*," we exhibit our innate human kindness, pity, and compassion.

The Greek base generates more technical and specialized words that refer to human beings as subjects of study or as objects of particular interest.

Important social studies words that are built on these bases include *humane, humanitarian, anthropologist, philanthropic,* and *anthropocentric.*

For a glossary of words with these roots, see the Digital Resource CD (filename: rootsglossary.pdf).

Name: _____ Date: _____

About the Root: World History:
The Rise of Humanism and the Humanities

Directions: Read the information. Then answer the questions.

> The Latin base *human-* and the Greek base *anthrop(o)-* mean "mankind," "human being." Many words from social studies contain these roots. Words built on Latin *human-* refer to human beings and the qualities of being human. These qualities may refer to human weakness, such as "to err is *human*," or to our more civilized features, such as "the *humane* thing to do." Words built on the Greek base *anthrop(o)-* are more technical and refer to human beings as subjects of study. *Anthropology*, for example, is the study of human societies.

◎ What kinds of things might a *humanitarian* do?

_____

◎ Explain the phrase "to err is *human*" in your own words.

_____

> As Europe emerged from the Middle Ages in the 14th and 15th centuries, a new philosophy called *Humanism* arose. Scholars came to believe that studying science and fostering the arts would allow human beings to find truth and goodness. They believed that our greatest resources were reason and intellect. The humanist movement led to a rebirth of interest in the ancient Greek and Roman cultures. We call this time the *Renaissance* (a French word meaning "rebirth").
>
>
>
> Renaissance scholars broadened education to include many subjects we still study in schools today. The *Humanities* include subjects such as language, literature, art, philosophy, and history. Humanists believed the Roman comedian Terence. Around 160 B.C., he said, "I am a human being. I consider everything human to be of interest to me!"

◎ Describe a scientific discovery or an artistic creation that is important to you on a separate sheet of paper.

◎ Do you think that science and the arts can help us find truth and goodness? Why or why not?

Name: _____ Date: _____

About the Root:
A Double Entendre: Habitat for Humanity

Directions: Read the information. Then answer the question.

Habitat for Humanity was founded in 1976. The organization builds houses for people in need in order to create "a world where everyone has a decent place to live." The name "Habitat for Humanity" plays on the two meanings of the word *humanity.* The phrase is a double entendre.

Volunteers build houses for people everywhere (i.e., for *humanity*). These homes are for people who have lost their homes because of poverty, war, or natural disasters. So the volunteers also construct habitats for *humanity* (i.e., out of human kindness for others). They consider building *human* habitats the *humane* thing to do!

Throughout history, people have responded *humanely* to relieve victims of natural disasters.

◎ What recent examples of *humanitarian relief* can you recall?

_____

_____

_____

_____

Name: _____   Date: _____

About the Root: World History:
The Anthropomorphic Gods of Greece

Directions: Read the information. Then answer the question.

Many ancient religions were polytheistic, but the ancient Greeks stood out as different in one important way. They believed that their gods looked like human beings. Other religions at the time represented gods as cats, birds, dogs, bulls, or snakes. But the Greek gods were portrayed as statues of beautiful men and women. They were *anthropomorphic,* or "human shaped."

But around 550 B.C., a philosopher-poet named Xenophanes (zeh-NAH-fu-neez) poked fun at the notion of the gods resembling human beings. He wrote, "If cows, horses, or lions had hands and could create things the way human beings do, horses would make their gods look like horses, and cows would make their gods look like cows. They would create images of the gods as having the same forms and bodies as their own!"

◎ Do you think that Xenophanes is critical of the gods themselves or of Greek attitudes toward the gods? Explain your thinking.

_____

_____

_____

_____

Name: _____ Date: _____

Divide and Conquer:
Being Human

Directions: Use the Base/Prefix Bank to help you identify the roots of the words below. Write the letter from the Definition Bank for the correct word.

Base/Prefix Bank

_in-_ = "not"   _morph-_ = "shape," "form"   _phil-_ = "love"

Definition Bank

A. kind, gentle, and compassionate

B. charitable; contributing money to charities

C. physically resembling a human being

D. a scholar or philosopher who studies human achievements

E. bloodthirsty and savage

Word	First Base/ Prefix Means	Second Base/ Suffix Means	Definition
1. philanthropic			
2. humane		X	
3. inhuman			
4. humanist		_-ist_ = one who believes in	
5. anthropomorphic			

Name: _____ Date: _____

Making Connections:
Who/What Am I?

· ·

Directions: Match each word in the first column with its speaker in the second column.

	Word		Speaker
_____	**1.** philanthropist	**A.**	I simply dislike people. Bah! Humbug!
_____	**2.** humanist	**B.**	I try to be kind to all people and everything around me on Earth.
_____	**3.** anthropologist	**C.**	I give a great deal of money to charities.
_____	**4.** misanthrope	**D.**	I can work endless hours without tiring.
_____	**5.** inhumane	**E.**	I study people who live in remote villages.
_____	**6.** humane	**F.**	I am not very nice at all. I can be quite cruel.
_____	**7.** superhuman	**G.**	I am a literary scholar.
_____	**8.** anthropoid	**H.**	While not human, I resemble one.

You Try It!

Use two of the words *humane, philanthropic,* or *anthropological* in your own sentences:

_____

_____

_____

_____

Bases *serv-*, *servat-* and *liber-*, *liberat-*

serv-, *servat-* = "keep," "save"

liber-, *liberat-* = "free"

Standards

Uses common, grade-appropriate Greek or Latin affixes and roots as clues to the meaning of a word

Determines the meaning of words and phrases as they are used in a text, including vocabulary specific to domains related to history/social studies

By the end of the year, reads and comprehends literary nonfiction in the grades 6–8 text complexity band proficiently, with scaffolding as needed at the high end of the range

Materials

- *About the Root: American History: Liberty* (page 125)

- *About the Root: Civics: What Does it Mean to Be Liberal or Conservative?* (page 126)

- *About the Root: World History: Liberation Theology* (page 127)

- *Divide and Conquer: To Keep, To Set Free* (page 128)

- *Making Connections: Role Playing* (page 129)

Teacher Preparation

- Read and review the background information about the bases *serv-*, *servat-* and *liber-*, *liberat-* on page 124 to familiarize yourself with their context in history and civics.

- Read and review the glossary of the bases found on the Digital Resource CD (filename: rootsglossary.pdf) for additional support.

Guided Practice

About the Root

1. Distribute copies of pages 125, 126, and/or 127 to students. Write *serv-*, *servat-* and *liber-*, *liberat-* and explain their meanings ("keep," "save," "free"). Ask partners to think about words they already know with these bases. Invite sharing.

2. Have students read the passages and answer the questions. Students can work independently or with partners. You may want to conclude with a whole-class discussion to review students' answers and reinforce the meaning of the roots in context.

Divide and Conquer

3. Distribute copies of *Divide and Conquer* (page 128). As you guide students through the activity page, use questions like these to generate discussion about each of the words:

- Where is the meaning of "keep," "save" or "free" in the word _____?

- Where might you see the word _____?

- Can you think of an example of _____?

Bases serv-, servat- and liber-, liberat- (cont.)

Making Connections

4. Distribute copies of *Making Connections* (page 129).

5. Divide the class into larger groups for acting or reading aloud. Then, have students complete the activity.

6. Conclude with a whole-class discussion that focuses on root meaning.

Words with serv-, servat- and liber-, liberat-

liberal	conservative
liberality	conservatory
liberate	conserve
liberation	observance
Liberia	observatory
libertarian	preservation
libertine	preservative
liberty	reservation
conservation	reserve
conservationist	reservoir
conservatism	

A list of words to print out for students can be found on the Digital Resource CD (filename: wordlists.pdf).

Spelling Hints:

The Latin base *serv-, servat* = "keep," "save," resembles another Latin base *(serv-, servit-)* in form but not in meaning. Words built on *serv-, servit-* have a base meaning of "serve," "slave," and are usually spelled with an *i* after the *v*. Examples include *servile*, *service*, *servitude*, and *subservient*. These words differ in core meaning from *serv, servat-* words, in which an *a* usually follows the *v*. Additionally, words built on the base *liber-, liberat-* do not have prefixes. They begin with the base.

Teacher Background Information and Tips

Latin Bases *serv-*, *servat-* = "keep," "save" and *liber-*, *liberat-* = "free"

The Latin base *serv-*, *servat-* means "keep," "save," and the Latin base *liber-* and *liberat-* means "free." These bases appear in many words in social studies and other content areas. These words describe political and cultural attitudes and practices (e.g., *conservatives, religious observances, historical preservation, liberals, liberation theology*). Words built on *liber-*, *liberat-* also arise in the study of American history (e.g., *Liberty Bell, Statue of Liberty, liberation movement, liberation of slaves, women's liberation, reservations, conservation*).

The Latin base *serv-*, *servat-* combines with many Latin prefixes in words whose core meaning centers on "keeping" things safe or "saved."

Important social studies words that are built on these bases include *conservatism, preservation, conservative, reservoir,* and *observatory.*

For a glossary of words with these roots, see the Digital Resource CD (filename: rootsglossary.pdf).

Name: _____ Date: _____

About the Root: American History:
Liberty

Directions: Read the information. Then answer the questions.

The Latin base *serv-, servat-* means "keep," "save." The Latin base *liber-* and *liberat-* means "free." These bases appear in many words in social studies and other content areas. The Latin base *serv-, servat-* combines with many Latin prefixes in words whose core meaning centers on "keeping" things safe or "saved." When we *preserve* historical records, for example, we "save" them from destruction and decay. People who hold *conservative* political views like to "keep," "save" things as they currently are.

Words built on *liber-, liberat-* are found in the study of American history. The original American colonies, for example, sought *liberation* from the British when they declared their independence in 1776. The American Civil War was fought in order to *liberate* the slaves of the Southern states. People who spend "freely" are called *liberal* spenders. In politics, people who hold *liberal* values often differ from *conservatives*.

Use the definitions of the roots to answer these questions.

◎ What does it mean to *conserve* natural resources?

_____

_____

◎ The Statue of *Liberty* is sometimes called *Lady Liberty*. What does this nickname mean?

_____

_____

_____

Name: _____ Date: _____

About the Root: Civics:

What Does it Mean to Be Liberal or Conservative?

Directions: Read the information. Then answer the question.

The answer to these questions may depend on whom you ask! With its base meaning of "free," *liberal* can mean generous and "freely" spending. People who spend money "freely" are *liberal* spenders. Some restaurants offer *liberal* portions. So, some think of *liberals* as wasting resources, since *liberal* spenders do not *conserve* their money. Some fiscal *conservatives* might view *liberals* in a negative light.

Conservatives like things to remain as they are. They want to keep traditions. They tend to support only minimal, gradual changes in society. Other people think it is a good thing to be free thinkers and to have *liberal* ideas. *Liberal* thinkers try not to be restricted by what others think. They try to be more broad-minded. But *conservatives* often disagree with such free-thinking attitudes.

Liberal politicians promote policies for social change. They want to expand opportunities to help the poor and improve the life of the common person. Social *liberals* are often contrasted with social *conservatives,* who prefer to keep policies the way they are. *Liberals* in politics tend to be progressive thinkers, whereas *conservatives* try to maintain traditions. It is even possible for the same person to be a social *liberal* and a fiscal *conservative.* To complicate matters, it's possible to be a *liberal conservative* or a *conservative liberal.* In each case, these are combinations of the values of one group with the stances of the other.

◎ Where do you stand? Are you more liberal, more conservative, or some combination? Explain your thinking.

_____

_____

_____

_____

_____

Name: _____ Date: _____

About the Root: World History:
Liberation Theology

Directions: Read the information. Then answer the questions.

As its name suggests, *liberation* theology stresses "freeing" people. The movement grew up in Latin America during the 1950s and 1960s. It arose because of social injustice and poverty. Roman Catholic priests began the movement, but it quickly attracted people from other faiths. Those who supported *liberation* theology believed that the church should work actively to free victims of poverty and oppression. The movement met with a mixed response. Some people embraced it. Others, however, rejected it because they believed that it emphasized political action over faith.

◎ Do you think religious groups should get involved in political action? Why or why not?

_____

_____

_____

_____

◎ Think about the word *liberation*, with its core meaning of "freedom." Can you think of other situations where the word *liberation* might be appropriate?

_____

_____

_____

_____

Name: _____   Date: _____

Divide and Conquer:
To Keep, To Set Free

Directions: Use the Base/Prefix Bank to help you identify the roots of the words below. Write the letter from the Definition Bank for the correct word.

Base/Prefix Bank

con- = "with," "together"   *pre-* = "before"   *re-* = "back," "again"

Definition Bank

A. to set free; to emancipate

B. the saving of something from decay or damage

C. a tract of public land set aside for special use or occupation

D. traditional; in favor of maintaining the status quo; resistant to change or progressivism

E. free and generous; progressive; not adhering to dogma or doctrine

Word	First Base/ Prefix Means	Second Base/ Suffix Means	Definition
1. conservative			
2. liberate		*-ate* = do, make (verb)	
3. liberal		*-al* = pertaining to (adjective)	
4. reservation			
5. preservation			

Name: _____　　Date: _____

Making Connections:
Role Playing
. . . .

Directions: Select one of the situations below. Prepare a short speech that shows your stance. You cannot use the words *for, against, liberal*, or *conservative* in your speech. Instead, find other ways to communicate your message. Give your speech to a group of classmates and ask them to read it. Then, ask them to tell what stance they think you have taken.

◎ You are for the conservation of natural resources.

◎ You are against the conservation of natural resources.

◎ You have conservative views about student dress in school.

◎ You have liberal views about student dress in school.

_____

_____

_____

_____

_____

_____

_____

_____

Bases *fid-, fidel-* and *cred-, credit-*

Standards

Uses common, grade-appropriate Greek or Latin affixes and roots as clues to the meaning of a word

Determines the meaning of words and phrases as they are used in a text, including vocabulary specific to domains related to history/social studies

By the end of the year, reads and comprehends literary nonfiction in the grades 6–8 text complexity band proficiently, with scaffolding as needed at the high end of the range

Materials

- *About the Root: United States History: The Marines, "Always Faithful"* (page 133)

- *About the Root: Man's Best Friend: High Fidelity* (page 134)

- *About the Root: World History: Credenzas in Ancient Rome* (page 135)

- *Divide and Conquer: Believe It or Not!* (page 136)

- *Making Connections: Crossword Puzzle* (page 137)

Teacher Preparation

- Read and review the background information about the bases *fid-, fidel-* and *credi-, credit-* on page 132 to familiarize yourself with their context in social studies and government.

- Read and review the glossary of the bases found on the Digital Resource CD (filename: rootsglossary.pdf) for additional support.

Guided Practice

About the Root

1. Distribute copies of pages 133, 134, and/or 135 to students. Write *fid-, fidel-* and *cred-, credit-* on the board and discuss their meanings ("faith," "trust," "believe"). Ask partners to think about words they already know with these bases. Invite whole-group sharing.

2. Have students read the passages and answer the questions. Students can work independently or with partners. You may want to conclude with a whole-class discussion to review students' answers and reinforce the meaning of the roots in context.

Divide and Conquer

3. Distribute copies of *Divide and Conquer* (page 136). As you guide students through the activity page, use questions like these to generate discussion about each of the words.

   - Where is the meaning of "faith," "trust" or "believe" in the word _____?

   - Where might you see the word _____?

   - Can you think of an example of _____?

Bases *fid-*, *fidel-* and *cred-*, *credit-* (cont.)

Making Connections

4. Distribute copies of *Making Connections* (page 137).

5. Allow students to work with partners to complete the crossword puzzle.

6. Conclude with a whole-class discussion that focuses on root meaning.

Words with *cred-*, *credit-* and *fid-*, *fidel-*

accredit	credo
accreditation	credulity
accredited	credulous
affidavit	creed
bonafide	diffidence
confidant	diffident
confidante	discredit
confide	fidelity
confidence	Fido
confident	incredible
confidential	incredulous
credence	infidel
credentials	infidelity
credenza	mala fide
credible	nullifidian
credibility	perfidious
credit	perfidy

A list of words to print out for students can be found on the Digital Resource CD (filename: wordlists.pdf).

Teacher Background Information and Tips

Bases *fid-, fidel-* = "faith," "trust" and *cred-, credit-* = "believe"

The Latin base *fid-, fidel-* means "faith," "trust," and the Latin base *cred-, credit-* means "believe." These two bases appear in social studies words describing trust, loyalty, belief, and faith. Such trust operates both between individuals (e.g., *marital fidelity, affidavit, credence, credible, credit*) and among groups or communities (e.g., *religious creed, accredited schools, fiduciary trusts, infidels, semper fidelis*).

Students may already know many words built on these bases, but they may not readily associate them with the base meanings of "faith," "trust" or "believe." For example, when we *confide* in friends, we share a "trust" "with" them. *Self-confident* people have a lot of "faith" in themselves, while *diffident* people do not. An old-fashioned name for a loyal dog is *Fido*. *Creditors* extend *credit cards* to consumers who buy *on credit*, "believing" that borrowers will pay their debts. *Incredible* stories "cannot" be "believed." The *credentials* (diplomas, licenses, certificates) that professionals display on office walls assure clients to "believe" that the workers in these offices are qualified.

> The word *infidel* requires sensitivity in the classroom. In some faiths, people who do not subscribe to a particular belief are called *infidels* (literally, people of "no" "faith" or "nonbelievers"; Latin prefix *in-* = "not"). In the Crusades of the Middle Ages, soldiers of the Christian Church invaded the Middle East to retrieve the Holy Land from the so-called Muslim *infidels*. Some Muslims, however, refer to Christians as *infidels* for not following the teachings of Mohammed. It may be worthwhile for students to reflect on this word. Ask, is a person who does not believe in our particular religion necessarily an *infidel*, a person of "no faith"? Depending on who is speaking, an *infidel* may be either a non-Christian or a non-Muslim.

Some *cred-, credit-* words refer to religious "beliefs." For example, worshipers declare their "belief" in a *creed*, also called a *credo*. Other words from this base suggest that *credit* must be earned before one can be "believed" as having met certain criteria. A student may earn *academic credit* or *extra credit* by passing tests, achieving certain grades, or completing work. A school must qualify to earn and retain its *accreditation* by the authorities. *Accredited* programs have met performance standards, resulting in authorities giving "belief" "to" them as academically valid (prefix *ac-* is assimilated *ad-* = "to," "toward," "add to").

For a glossary of words with these roots, see the Digital Resource CD (filename: rootsglossary.pdf).

Name: _____ Date: _____

About the Root: United States History:
The Marines, "Always Faithful"

Directions: Read the information. Then answer the questions.

> The Latin base *fid-, fidel-* means "faith," "trust," and the Latin base *cred-, credit-* means "believe." These two bases appear in words describing trust, loyalty, belief, and faith. Trust may be between individuals (e.g., *marital fidelity, affidavit, credit*) and among groups or communities (e.g., *religious creed, accredited schools*).

◎ How does *confiding* in someone show faith or trust?

_____

_____

◎ How does the word *credit* include the idea of belief?

_____

_____

> The United States Marine Corps adopted a new motto in 1883. They selected a Latin phrase, *semper fidelis*. In fact, the official march of the United States Marine Corps is also called *Semper Fidelis*. The famous composer John Philip Sousa wrote the march while he was the director of the Marine Band.
>
> The motto, which means "always faithful," is abbreviated as *semper fi*. When a person joins the Marines, he or she does so for life. After active service, a Marine first enters the reserves and then the ranks of Retired Marines. Throughout life, Marines can be called on to return to duty. Once a Marine, always a Marine. There is no such thing as an ex-Marine. That is why they say, *"semper fi*, always faithful—to the mission, to the Corps, to the country."

◎ In what ways do Marines display their *fidelity* to the country?

_____

_____

◎ What do you think about *Semper Fi* as a motto? Explain your thinking on a separate sheet of paper.

Name: _____ Date: _____

About the Root: Man's Best Friend:
High Fidelity

Directions: Read the information. Then answer the question.

The Victor Talking Machine Company produced the Victrola Gramophone (an early type of record player) in the early 1900s. They bragged that their machine had "high *fidelity*" because the music it played sounded as good as if you were hearing it live. Ads for the new machine showed a dog listening to a speaker horn. The horn looked like a megaphone. With head tilted and ears perked, the dog sat patiently by the speaker, thinking that "his master's voice" was coming directly from the machine.

This image captured the essence of high *fidelity*, trustworthiness in the reproduction of sound. Of all animals, the dog—also called man's best friend—is synonymous with loyalty and trustworthiness. Like the Victrola, dogs also have high *fidelity* to their masters.

The advertisers were clever, weren't they? By showing a trusty dog next to the record player, they promoted their new sound system as the latest thing in "high fidelity."

◎ Today, we apply the word *fidelity* to a number of situations. Can you think of a situation in which the word *fidelity* might be appropriate?

_____

_____

_____

_____

_____

_____

Name: _____ Date: _____

About the Root: World History:
Credenzas in Ancient Rome

Directions: Read the information. Then answer the question.

During the Roman Empire, the emperor had to protect himself against enemies who wanted to kill him and seize the throne. When he left his palace, he always had bodyguards around him. But at home, there was a constant danger that someone might poison his food.

Because of this, the emperor appointed slaves to taste his food before serving it to him. The food was placed on a side-table called a *credenza*. As the servant would taste each dish, he would declare, "I believe (*credo*) this dish is safe." But *credenzas* were not foolproof. In 54 A.D., the Emperor Claudius died from eating a poisonous plate of his favorite food—mushrooms.

Today, a *credenza* can be found in well-furnished offices. It is a short and wide cabinet that often matches the executive's desk. This cabinet contributes to prestige; the modern boss has the same kind of furniture as a Roman emperor!

◎ The word *credenza* is built on the same base as the words *credible*, *incredible*, and *credentials*. What *credentials* do you think an ancient Roman food-tester needed to have in order to be *credible*?

_____
_____
_____
_____
_____
_____

Name: _____ Date: _____

Divide and Conquer:
Believe It or Not!

. . . .

Directions: Use the Base/Prefix Bank to help you identify the roots of the words below. *X* means the word does not have that element. Write the letter from the Definition Bank for the correct word.

Base/Prefix Bank

bon(a)- = "good"   *in-* = "not"   *semper-* = "always"

Definition Bank

A. a statement or confessional declaration of firmly held beliefs

B. a non-believer; someone who has no faith in a particular religion

C. unbelievable

D. genuine, sincere; made or extended in good faith

E. motto of the United States Marine Corps: "Always Faithful"

Word	First Base/ Prefix Means	Second Base/ Suffix Means	Definition
1. infidel			
2. bona fide			
3. semper fidelis			
4. creed		X	
5. incredible			

Name: _____ Date: _____

Making Connections:
Crossword Puzzle

Directions: Use the words in the Word Bank and the clues to complete the crossword puzzle below.

Word Bank

confidant	confidence	confident	credible
creditor	fidelity	Fido	incredible

Across

1. As I have practiced the piano, my _____ has grown.

5. Her story made sense. We all believed it was _____.

6. I am _____ that I will get an A on my test.

7. It seemed _____, but the story was actually true.

Down

1. My best friend is my _____.

2. Our most important _____ is the mortgage company.

3. Our dog _____ is very loyal.

4. _____ is an important quality in a friend.

Bases *bell-* and *pac-*

bell- = "war"

pac- = "peace"

Standards

Uses common, grade-appropriate Greek or Latin affixes and roots as clues to the meaning of a word

Determines the meaning of words and phrases as they are used in a text, including vocabulary specific to domains related to history/social studies

By the end of the year, reads and comprehends literary nonfiction in the grades 6–8 text complexity band proficiently, with scaffolding as needed at the high end of the range

Materials

- *About the Root: War and Peace* (page 141)

- *About the Root: World History: Rebels and Rebellions* (page 142)

- *About the Root: Ancient History: The Pax Romana* (page 143)

- *Divide and Conquer: Make Peace, Not War* (page 144)

- *Making Connections: Who/What Are We?* (page 145)

Teacher Preparation

- Read and review the background information about the bases *bell-* and *pac-* on page 140 to familiarize yourself with their context in social studies.

- Read and review the glossary of the bases found on the Digital Resource CD (filename: rootsglossary.pdf) for additional support.

Guided Practice

About the Root

1. Distribute copies of pages 141, 142, and/or 143 to students. Write *bell-* and *pac-* on the board and explain their meanings ("war," "peace"). Ask partners to think about words they already know with these bases. Invite sharing.

2. Have students read the passages and answer the questions. Students can work independently or with partners. You may want to conclude with a whole-class discussion to review students' answers and reinforce the meaning of the roots in context.

Divide and Conquer

3. Distribute copies of *Divide and Conquer* (page 144). As you guide students through the activity page, use questions like these to generate discussion about each of the words:

   - Where is the meaning of "peace" or "war" in the word _____?

   - Where might you see the word _____?

   - Can you think of an example of _____?

Bases *bell-* and *pac-* (cont.)

Making Connections

4. Distribute copies of *Making Connections* (page 145).

5. Have students read all of the definitions before completing the activity sheet.

6. Conclude with a whole-class discussion that focuses on root meaning.

Words with *bell-* and *pac-*

antebellum	rebellion
bellicose	rebellious
belligerence	pacific
belligerent	Pacific Ocean
casus belli	pacifism
postbellum	pacifist
post bellum	pacify
rebel	pact

A list of words to print out for students can be found on the Digital Resource CD (filename: wordlists.pdf).

Spelling Hints:

As Latin bases, when *pac-* and *bell-* are at the beginning of a word, they are normally followed by a connecting *i*, which links them to the next base or suffix. Hence, such spellings as *pacify, pacific, bellicose, belligerence,* etc.

Teacher Background Information and Tips

Bases *bell-* = "war" and *pac-* = "peace"

The Latin bases meaning "war" (*bell-*) and "peace" (*pac-*) appear in social studies words referring to events from world history. In American history, *antebellum* refers to the period before the Civil War (War Between the States, 1861–1865), while the *postbellum* reconstruction took place after the Civil War (**Note:** both

ante bellum and *post bellum* may also be written as two-word phrases). In a *rebellion*, people engage in a "war," fighting "back" against those in power (i.e., they *rebel*). In 1899–1900, Chinese nationalists staged the Boxer *Rebellion*; they fought back against the foreigners who were in control of the government.

The *casus belli* (a Latin phrase used as English; Latin *casus* means "event," "occasion") is the event or occasion that triggers a war. The *casus belli* of World War I, for example, was the assassination of Archduke Ferdinand in 1914. The underlying causes of war are generally rooted in fundamental and long-standing conflicts. The *casus belli*, while not the actual reason for the war, is the single event that brings these conflicts to a head.

The base *pac-* appears in such words as *pacifist* (literally, a "peace-maker") and *pacify*. The *Pacific Ocean* received its name in 1520 from Portuguese explorer Ferdinand Magellan, impressed by its calm and "peaceful" waters in contrast to the choppy Atlantic. The adjective *pacific* means "conciliatory," "making peace," as in the phrase, "*pacific* measures" (the suffixes *-(i)fy*, *-(i)fic* mean "make," "do").

Important social studies words built on these bases include *antebellum*, *rebellion*, *bellicose*, *pacify*, and *pacifism*.

For a glossary of words with these roots, see the Digital Resource CD (filename: rootsglossary.pdf).

Name: _____   Date: _____

About the Root:
War and Peace

· ·

Directions: Read the information. Then answer the questions.

The Latin bases meaning "war" (*bell-*) and "peace" (*pac-*) appear in social studies words referring to events from American and world history. In American history, the word *antebellum* usually refers to the time before the Civil War. In a *rebellion*, people engage in a "war" to fight "back" against those in power. *Pacifists,* by contrast, are literally "peacemakers." In 1520, Portuguese explorer Ferdinand Magellan was so impressed by the "peaceful" waters of the ocean he discovered that he named it the *Pacific* Ocean.

◎ What is the *postbellum* period?

_____

_____

_____

_____

◎ How does the word *pacify* mean to cause "peace" in someone?

_____

_____

_____

_____

Name: _____ Date: _____

About the Root: World History:
Rebels and Rebellions

· ·

Directions: Read the information. Then answer the questions.

Are you a *rebel*? A *rebel* is someone who goes against authority. *Rebels* do not like accepted ways of doing things. In the late 1960s, for example, individual young people *rebelled* against many social customs.

Sometimes, groups band together to oppose authority or the accepted ways of doing things. When this happens, they start a *rebellion*. *Rebellions* are usually aimed against the government or other authorities currently in power. In early American history, for example, the British believed that the Revolutionary War waged by the colonists was a *rebellion*.

Rebellions do not need to be war related. The *Whiskey Rebellion* was in 1790. A group of farmers refused to pay taxes on their corn, which was used to make whiskey. In 1900, the *Boxer Rebellion* in China aimed to create a stronger government by driving foreigners out of the country. All *rebellions* hope to replace part or all of established authority.

◎ What were some of things against which the early American colonists *rebelled*?

_____

_____

_____

◎ The British rulers called the uprising of the colonists a *rebellion*. But the Americans called it a *revolution*. Which word sounds more negative? Why do you think this is so?

_____

_____

_____

_____

Name: _____ Date: _____

About the Root: Ancient History:
The Pax Romana

. . . .

Directions: Read the information. Then answer the question.

When Caesar Augustus became Emperor of Rome in 27 B.C., he dedicated statues and temples to a goddess named *Pax*, meaning "peace." After years of civil war, Rome had finally found peace at home and abroad. The Augustan Peace, *Pax Augusta*, was at last a reality!

Over time, this peace spread to the entire empire and came to be known as the *Pax Romana*, "the Roman Peace." But a Roman historian named Tacitus was skeptical. Just because tribes in Europe were no longer *rebelling* against the invincible Roman troops, he argued, did not necessarily mean they were at peace, especially after the Roman army had ruined their lands. Tacitus seemed to believe that this peace was no peace at all. He wrote of the Roman army, "Where they make a desert, they call it peace."

◎ Is the absence of conflict the same thing as peace? Explain your thinking.

_____

_____

_____

_____

_____

_____

_____

_____

Name: _____ Date: _____

Divide and Conquer:
Make Peace, Not War

Directions: Use the Base/Prefix Bank to help you identify the roots of the words below. Write the letter from the Definition Bank for the correct word.

Base/Prefix Bank

ante- = "before"   *-ific* = "making," "doing"
-ify = "make," "do"   *re-* = "back," "again"

Definition Bank

A. hostile; engaged in war

B. an uprising

C. conciliatory; aiming to make peace

D. to calm or appease

E. the time period preceding or before a war (especially the American Civil War)

Word	First Base/ Prefix Means	Second Base/ Suffix Means	Definition
1. pacify			
2. antebellum			
3. belligerent		*ger-* = to wage	
4. pacific			
5. rebellion			

Name: _____   Date: _____

Making Connections:
Who/What Are We?

Directions: Match each word or phrase in the first column with its speaker in the second column.

Word/Phrase	Speaker
_____ 1. a bellicose act	**A.** We are talks which seek to resolve conflict between nations.
_____ 2. rebellions	**B.** We carry signs that say, "Make peace, not war."
_____ 3. antebellum south	**C.** We are uprisings against an unjust government.
_____ 4. pacific measures	**D.** Our economy was largely based on slave labor.
_____ 5. rebels	**E.** We carry signs that say, "Fight back!" We challenge all authority.
_____ 6. pacifists	**F.** I am an unprovoked invasion of a neighboring country.
_____ 7. casus belli	**G.** I am the event that triggered a war.

You Try It!

Use two of the words *belligerent, pacify,* or *rebellious* in your own sentences:

_____

_____

_____

_____

_____

Base *annu-, enni-*

annu-, enni- = "year"

Standards

Uses common, grade-appropriate Greek or Latin affixes and roots as clues to the meaning of a word

Determines the meaning of words and phrases as they are used in a text, including vocabulary specific to domains related to history/social studies

By the end of the year, reads and comprehends literary nonfiction in the grades 6–8 text complexity band proficiently, with scaffolding as needed at the high end of the range

Materials

- *About the Root: Year After Year* (page 149)

- *About the Root: Culture and Society: Can You Count in Latin?* (page 150)

- *About the Root: United States History: The Bicentennial* (page 151)

- *Divide and Conquer: How Many Years?* (page 152)

- *Making Connections: What Am I?* (page 153)

Teacher Preparation

- Read and review the background information about the base *annu-, enni-* on page 148 to familiarize yourself with their context in history, culture, and society.

- Read and review the glossary of the base found on the Digital Resource CD (filename: rootsglossary.pdf) for additional support.

Guided Practice

About the Root

1. Distribute copies of pages 149, 150, and/or 151 to students. Write *annu-* and *enni-* on the board and discuss their meaning ("year"). Ask partners to think about words they already know with this base. Follow with a brief discussion.

2. Have students read the remaining passages and answer the questions. Students can work independently or with partners. You may want to conclude with a whole-class discussion to review students' answers and reinforce the meaning of the roots in context.

Divide and Conquer

3. Distribute copies of *Divide and Conquer* (page 152). As you guide students through the activity page, use questions like these to generate discussion about each of the words:

- Where is the meaning of "year" in the word _____?

- Where might you see the word _____?

- Can you think of an example of _____?

Base *annu-, enni-* (cont.)

Making Connections

4. Distribute copies of *Making Connections* (page 153).

5. Have students read all of the definitions before completing the activity sheet.

6. Conclude with a whole-class discussion that focuses on root meaning.

Words with *annu-, enni-*

annalist

annals

anniversary

annual

annuity

biannual

bicentennial

biennial

biennium

centennial

millennium

perennial

quadrennial

quadrennium

semiannual

sesquicentennial

A list of words to print out for students can be found on the Digital Resource CD (filename: wordlists.pdf).

Spelling Hints:

All words based on *annu-* and *enni-* are spelled with two *n*'s. Additionally, since both forms of the base combine with numerical bases (also called numerical prefixes), we list derivatives in two lists: one with *annu-* words and one with *enni-* words. Note that words deriving from the form *annu-* may have dropped the *u* (e.g., *anniversary*).

Teacher Background Information and Tips

Base *annu-, enni-* = "year"

The Latin base *annu-, enni-*, meaning "year," generates a large number of words related to the study of history. Students may already know general-usage words from this base, such as *annual, anniversary,* and *millennium.* This base also appears in academic vocabulary referring to governmental terms of office and elections (e.g., *biennial, quadrennial*), to celebrations of communities and countries which are 100 years old or more (e.g., *centennial, sesquicentennial, bicentennial*), and to historical records called *annals.*

In recording historical dates, we traditionally use the abbreviations B.C. ("Before Christ") and A.D. (*Anno Domini,* "In the Year of the Lord"). In more recent professional writing, however, many historians and scholars are replacing the abbreviation B.C. with B.C.E. ("Before the Common Era"), and A.D. with C.E. ("Common Era"). The abbreviations B.C.E. and C.E. are viewed as nonconfessional, or in other words, neutral on the Christian doctrine that Christ is the Lord.

The two forms of the Latin base *annu-, enni-* can be distinguished as follows: the form *annu-* is used in words describing a single year or a partial year (e.g., *annual, biannual,* or *semiannual*), whereas the form *enni-* is used in words describing multiples of years (e.g., *perennial, biennial, centennial,* and *millennium*).

Important social studies words that are built on this base include *anniversary, biannual, annuity,* and *millennium.*

For a glossary of words with this root, see the Digital Resource CD (filename: rootsglossary.pdf).

Name: _____ Date: _____

About the Root:
Year After Year

· ·

Directions: Read the information. Then answer the questions.

The Latin base *annu-, enni-* means "year." This base is part of many words related to the study of history. It is also part of words like *annual* and *anniversary*.

The form *annu-* is used in words referring to a single year or to a partial year (for example, *annual*, *anniversary*, or *semiannual*). The form *enni-* is used in words referring to multiples of years (for example, *biennial*, *centennial*, or *perennial*).

◎ How does *annual* mean "year"?

_____

_____

◎ How does *anniversary* mean "year"?

_____

_____

◎ Historical records are sometimes called *annals*. How does this word mean "year"?

_____

_____

◎ The president of the United States serves a *quadrennial* term. How many years are in a *quadrennium*? How do you know?

_____

_____

_____

_____

Name: _____ Date: _____

About the Root: Culture and Society:
Can You Count in Latin?

Directions: Read the information. Then answer the question.

Did you know that if you know some Latin roots, you can count in Latin? A *centennial* celebration marks 100 years. In this long word, you recognize the base *enni-*, meaning "year." You probably also know that *cent-* means 100. Think of other *cent-* words and how they mean 100: there are 100 *cents* in a dollar, 100 years in a *century*, and up to 100 legs on a *centipede*. So, can you figure out how many years are in a *bicentennial*?

Can you figure out how many years are in a *sesquicentennial*? Look at the Latin and do the math! If the Latin prefix *sesqui-* means "one and a half," how much is one and one-half times 100 years? Check your answer in a dictionary by looking up *sesquicentennial*!

◎ How many years are in a *bicentennial*? In a *sesquicentennial*? In a *tricentennial*? How do you know you are right?

_____

_____

_____

_____

_____

_____

_____

_____

_____

_____

_____

Name: _____   Date: _____

About the Root: United States History:
The Bicentennial

Directions: Read the information. Then answer the questions.

July 4, 1976, was the culmination of a long celebration for the United States. That day marked the 200th anniversary of the signing of the Declaration of Independence. So it was chosen as the day to celebrate America's *bicentennial* birthday.

Planning for the bicentennial began in the mid-1960s. Special coins were minted. A "Freedom Train" visited each of the lower 48 states. Many political figures, including President Gerald Ford, gave speeches about important events in the nation's history. Tall ships floated in harbors on the East Coast. People were encouraged to paint mailboxes and fire hydrants red, white, and blue. And of course—fireworks! Lots and lots of fireworks! All this celebration paid tribute to the founding of the country.

◎ Why do you think planning the *bicentennial* took so long?

_____

_____

_____

_____

◎ If the birthday of the United States is July 4, 1776, when will we celebrate our *tricentennial*? How do you know?

_____

_____

_____

_____

_____

Name: _____ Date: _____

Divide and Conquer:
How Many Years?

Directions: Use the Base/Prefix Bank to help you identify the roots of the words below. *X* means the word does not contain that element. Write the letter from the Definition Bank for the correct word.

Base/Prefix Bank

per- = "through"   *quadr-* = "four"

mill- = "thousand"   *vers-* = "turn"

Definition Bank

A. lasting four years or occurring every four years

B. a yearly celebration or observance

C. a period of 1,000 years

D. historical records

E. recurrent; enduring over many years

Word	First Base/ Prefix Means	Second Base/ Suffix Means	Definition
1. quadrennial			
2. perennial			
3. anniversary			
4. annals		X	
5. millennium			

Name: _____ Date: _____

Making Connections:
What Am I?

. . . .

Directions: Match each word in the first column with its speaker in the second column.

	Word		Speaker
_____	**1.** millennium	**A.**	I am a 150-year anniversary.
_____	**2.** bicentennial	**B.**	My elections take place every four years.
_____	**3.** centennial	**C.**	I am a 200-year anniversary.
_____	**4.** quadrennial	**D.**	I come around every six months (**Hint:** 6 months = $\frac{1}{2}$ year)
_____	**5.** biannual	**E.**	I am a 100-year anniversary.
_____	**6.** biennial	**F.**	I am a term that lasts two years.
_____	**7.** sesquicentennial	**G.**	I come around two times a year.
_____	**8.** semiannual	**H.**	I last 1,000 years.

You Try It!

Use two of the words *perennial, annual,* or *annals* in your own sentences:

_____

_____

_____

_____

Base *stru-, struct-*

stru-, struct- = "build"

Standards

Uses common, grade-appropriate Greek or Latin affixes and roots as clues to the meaning of a word

Determines the meaning of words and phrases as they are used in a text, including vocabulary specific to domains related to history/social studies

By the end of the year, reads and comprehends literary nonfiction in the grades 6–8 text complexity band proficiently, with scaffolding as needed at the high end of the range

Materials

- *About the Root: United States History: A House Divided* (page 157)

- *About the Root: American History: The Obstruction of Justice* (page 158)

- *About the Root: World History: All Roads Lead to Rome* (page 159)

- *Divide and Conquer: Taking Apart Building Words* (page 160)

- *Making Connections: Let's Build Words* (page 161)

Teacher Preparation

- Read and review the background information about the base *stru-, struct-* on page 156 to familiarize yourself with their context in social studies.

- Read and review the glossary of the base found on the Digital Resource CD (filename: rootsglossary.pdf) for additional support.

Guided Practice

About the Root

1. Distribute copies of pages 157, 158, and/or 159 to students. Write *stru-*, and *struct-* on the board and discuss their meaning ("build"). Ask partners to think about words they already know with this base. Invite whole-group conversation.

2. Have students read the remaining passages and answer the questions. Students can work independently or with partners. You may want to conclude with a whole-class discussion to review students' answers and reinforce the meaning of the roots in context.

Divide and Conquer

3. Distribute copies of *Divide and Conquer* (page 160). As you guide students through the activity page, use questions like these to generate discussion about each of the words:

   - Where is the meaning of "build" in the word _____?

   - Where might you see the word _____?

   - Can you think of an example of _____?

Base *stru-, struct-* (cont.)

Making Connections

4. Distribute copies of *Making Connections* (page 161).

5. Have students work with partners to complete the activity. After partners have worked on the chart, invite whole-group sharing. You might want to make one big chart to compile students' answers. This could be posted in the classroom.

6. Conclude with a whole-class discussion that focuses on root meaning.

Words with *stru-, struct-*

construct
construe
deconstruct
deconstruction
destroy
destruct
destruction
indestructible
infrastructure
instruct
instruction
instructor
instrument
instrumental
misconstrue
obstruct
obstruction
reconstruct
reconstruction
reconstructive
structure
substructure
superstructure

A list of words to print out for students can be found on the Digital Resource CD (filename: wordlists.pdf).

Teacher Background Information and Tips

Base *stru-*, *struct-* = "build"

The Latin base *stru-*, *struct-*, meaning "build," appears in many social studies words. World history records many events in which the *destruction* of one country by another is followed by *reconstruction*. The Latin base *stru-*, *struct-* carries the nuanced meaning of building through careful arranging and sequencing. A house, for example, is *constructed* one step at a time, starting with the foundation and then proceeding upward. When we *construe* our thoughts into a coherent sentence, we do so methodically and thoughtfully.

This base carries the literal meaning of "build," in such words as *construction site* (where actual "building" takes place); *infrastructure* (referring to roads, bridges, subways, and other *structures* "built" to facilitate transportation); the *substructure* of a building on which the *superstructure* is imposed; an *obstruction* in the road that blocks traffic or the flow of water (e.g., an *obstruction* in a drain); and the *destruction* of a building.

This base also carries the figurative meaning of "build," without reference to physical building, in such words and phrases as *obstruction of justice* (in which a person figuratively blocks an investigation); the *Reconstruction of the South* (after the end of the American Civil War in 1865); the *restructuring* of a government or business; and the *instruction* of students in school (which aims, figuratively, to shape and "build" them). The figurative phrase *constructive criticism* describes comments that "build up" the student to enable him or her to produce an improved paper or project. Negative remarks that knock "down" and destroy are called *destructive criticism* or *destructive comments*.

The words *construct, construction,* and *constructive* (Latin prefix *con-* = "with," "together") are often preceded by additional prefixes. To *reconstruct* is to "construct" or "build together" again (Latin prefix *re-* = "back," "again"). To *deconstruct* is to take apart methodically, piece by piece (literally, to undo a construction; Latin prefix *de-* = "down," "off"). To *misconstrue* one's words or ideas is to "build" them "together" "wrongly" (prefix *mis-* = "wrongly," "in error").

The base *stru-*, *struct-* combines with the prefix *in-* to describe the preparation of an army for battle (Latin *instruo* means "prepare an army for battle"). This is the origin of the word *instruction,* referring originally to the arranging and "building up" of troops and informing them which strategies and battle formations to employ.

For a glossary of words with this root, see the Digital Resource CD (filename: rootsglossary.pdf).

Name: _____ Date: _____

About the Root: United States History:

A House Divided

· ·

Directions: Read the information. Then answer the questions.

> The Latin base *stru-*, *struct,* means "build." It appears in many words in social studies. Sometimes, the "build" in *stru-*, *struct-* words is literal. War may lead to the *destruction* of a country, for example.

◎ The Latin prefix *de-*means "down." Use the base *struct-* and this prefix to explain how the word *destruction* has something to do with "build."

_____

_____

> Sometimes, the "build" in *stru-*, *struct-* words is figurative. It refers to the idea of building but not actual structures. For example, the period following the Civil War is often called *Reconstruction.*

◎ *Re-* means "back" or "again." Use this to explain how *reconstruction* has something to do with "build."

_____

_____

> On June 16, 1858, three hours after receiving the Republican nomination for the United States Senate, Abraham Lincoln delivered his famous "House Divided Speech." Lincoln was disturbed that slavery still existed in the Southern states. He wondered how the United States could consider itself a "Union" when half of the states still held slaves. In his remarks, he said, "A house divided against itself cannot stand. I believe this government cannot endure permanently half slave and half free. I do not expect the Union to be dissolved—I do not expect the house to fall—but I do expect it will cease to be divided. It will become all one thing or all the other."
>
> In another three years, Civil War would break out, dividing the United States. After the war ended, in 1865, the great task of *Reconstruction* began. The "divided house" had to be put together again.

◎ Why do you think Lincoln compared the nation to a house? Do you think this comparison worked well? Write your thoughts on a separate sheet of paper.

Name: _____   Date: _____

About the Root: American History:
The Obstruction of Justice

Directions: Read the information. Then answer the questions.

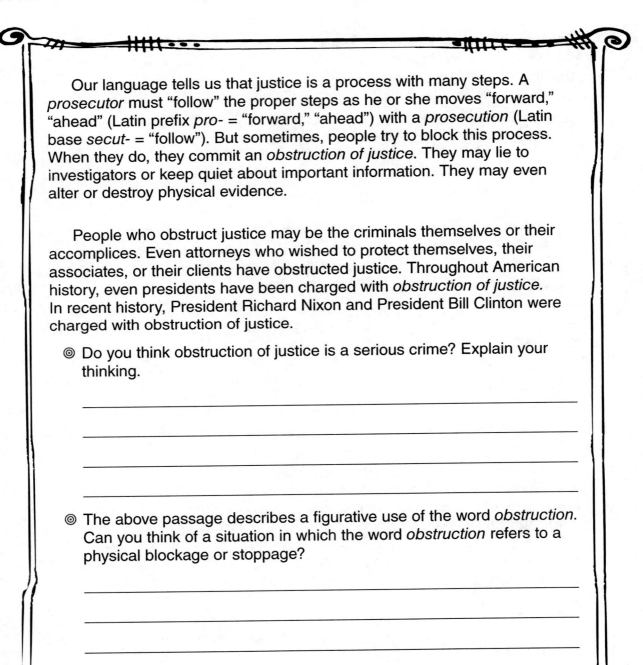

Our language tells us that justice is a process with many steps. A *prosecutor* must "follow" the proper steps as he or she moves "forward," "ahead" (Latin prefix *pro-* = "forward," "ahead") with a *prosecution* (Latin base *secut-* = "follow"). But sometimes, people try to block this process. When they do, they commit an *obstruction of justice.* They may lie to investigators or keep quiet about important information. They may even alter or destroy physical evidence.

People who obstruct justice may be the criminals themselves or their accomplices. Even attorneys who wished to protect themselves, their associates, or their clients have obstructed justice. Throughout American history, even presidents have been charged with *obstruction of justice.* In recent history, President Richard Nixon and President Bill Clinton were charged with obstruction of justice.

◎ Do you think obstruction of justice is a serious crime? Explain your thinking.

_____

_____

_____

_____

◎ The above passage describes a figurative use of the word *obstruction.* Can you think of a situation in which the word *obstruction* refers to a physical blockage or stoppage?

_____

_____

_____

_____

Name: _____ Date: _____

About the Root: World History:
All Roads Lead to Rome

Directions: Read the information. Then answer the questions.

The ancient Romans set out to include all of Europe in their empire. But they found the going hard. There were no good roads leading from Italy, across the Alps, and into France and Germany. The pathways were dirt roads, often washed out by heavy rains. This left the soldiers ankle-deep in mud as they marched with their heavy equipment.

But the Romans were excellent engineers and soon solved the problem. They developed an elaborate *infrastructure* of roads. They first poured a foundation of stones and gravel. Then they built the road on top, slightly above ground level. They even made the roads rise slightly in the middle so that rainwater would flow off the road instead of collecting in the middle.

The Romans believed that their city was eternal. "Rome, the Eternal City" was their motto. They therefore set their *infrastructures* to last forever. Some of the original Roman roads and their foundations are still in use today, 2,000 years later! Even in modern America, we follow the Roman tradition of laying an *infrastructure* and then building a highway system on top. In fact, that is why we call those roads *highways*. They are built on *infrastructures* that lie underneath.

◎ What is the advantage of having *infrastructure* beneath a road?

_____

_____

_____

◎ The Romans were great builders. Can you name any other constructions, aside from roads, for which they are known?

_____

_____

_____

Name: _____ Date: _____

Divide and Conquer:
Taking Apart Building Words

Directions: Use the Base/Prefix Bank to help you identify the roots of the words below. Write the letter from the Definition Bank for the correct word. **Note:** Two of the words have two prefixes.

Base/Prefix Bank

con- = "with," "together"   *infra-* = "underneath,"   *ob-* = "up against"
mis- = "wrongly," "error"   "beneath," "below"   *re-* = "back," "again"

Definition Bank

A. a building; the act of building

B. misunderstand

C. reassemble, rebuild

D. block or impede

E. permanent groundwork for a transportation system

Word	First Base/ Prefix Means	Second Base/ Suffix Means		Definition
1. construction				
2. infrastructure				
3. obstruct				
4. misconstrue				
5. reconstruct				

Name: _____ Date: _____

Making Connections:
Let's Build Words

Directions: Work with a partner. Fill in the chart with as many *stru-* and *struct-* words as you can. Share your answers with your partner, and explain your thinking.

Suffixes/Prefixes	None	-er/-or	-ion	-ure
None				
con-				
de-				
infra-				
re-				
super-				
More than 1 prefix				

Base grad-, gress-

grad-, gress- = "step," "go"

Standards

Uses common, grade-appropriate Greek or Latin affixes and roots as clues to the meaning of a word

Determines the meaning of words and phrases as they are used in a text, including vocabulary specific to domains related to history/social studies

By the end of the year, reads and comprehends literary nonfiction in the grades 6–8 text complexity band proficiently, with scaffolding as needed at the high end of the range

Materials

- *About the Root: Civics: Congress* (page 165)

- *About the Root: Economics: Progressive and Regressive Taxes* (page 166)

- *About the Root: Politics: The Diversity of Political Views* (page 167)

- *Divide and Conquer: Gradual Progress* (page 168)

- *Making Connections: Who/What Am I?* (page 169)

Teacher Preparation

- Read and review the background information about the base *grad-*, *gress-* on page 164 to familiarize yourself with its context in civics, economics, and politics.

- Read and review the glossary of the base found on the Digital Resource CD (filename: rootsglossary.pdf) for additional support.

Guided Practice

About the Root

1. Distribute copies of pages 165, 166, and/or 167 to students. Write *grad-* and *gress-* on the board and discuss their meanings ("step," "go"). Ask partners to think about words they already know with this base. Invite sharing.

2. Have students read the passages and answer the questions. Students can work independently or with partners. You may want to conclude with a whole-class discussion to review students' answers and reinforce the meaning of the roots in context.

Divide and Conquer

3. Distribute copies of *Divide and Conquer* (page 168). As you guide students through the activity page, use questions like these to generate discussion about each of the words:

   - Where is the meaning of "step" or "go" in the word _____?

   - Where might you see the word _____?

   - Can you think of an example of _____?

Base grad-, gress- (cont.)

Making Connections

4. Distribute copies of *Making Connections* (page 169).

5. Have students read all of the definitions before completing the activity sheet.

6. Conclude with a whole-class discussion that focuses on root meaning.

Words with grad-, gress-

aggression
aggressive
aggressor
centigrade
congress
congressional
digress
digression
digressive
egress
grade
gradient
gradual
graduate
progress
progressive
regress
regression
regressive
transgress
transgression
transgressor

A list of words to print out for students can be found on the Digital Resource CD (filename: wordlists.pdf).

Teacher Background Information and Tips

Base *grad-*, *gress-* = "step," "go"

The Latin base *grad-*, *gress-*, meaning "step," "go," appears in many general usage words that students may already know and in words from social studies. Most words from this base refer to figurative, not literal, "stepping." When we work *gradually*, for example, we proceed one "step" at a time—but without actually walking! Student *grades* of A, B, C, D are arranged in "steps," as are the *grade* levels of *first grade, second grade,* and so on. When students *graduate*, they "step" up to the next *grade* in the sequence. Even the *grades* of sandpaper advance "step by step" as they are refined, from *coarse grade* to *medium grade* to *fine grade*. A *centigrade* thermometer has 100 degrees, or demarcated "steps," of temperature from freezing to boiling.

The form *grad-* is usually found at the beginning of a word. Most *grad-* words do not begin with prefixes. The form *gress-*, by contrast, is always preceded by a directional prefix, which indicates the direction of the figurative "stepping" or "going." *Congress*, for example, consists of legislators who "step" "together" as they make laws (Latin prefix *con-* = "with," "together"). *Progress* is "forward" movement (Latin prefix *pro-* = "forward," "ahead"), while *regression* is a "step" "back" to an earlier behavior (Latin prefix *re-* = "back," "again"). To *digress* is to wander or stray from the main topic while speaking or writing (Latin prefix *di-* = "apart," "in different directions"; literally, to "step" "apart" from the topic). An act of military *aggression* consists of an unprovoked attack against an opponent (Latin prefix *ad-* assimilated as *ag-* = "to," "toward," "add to"; literally, a "stepping" "toward" an opponent with hostile intent). A *transgression* is a moral offense, a "stepping" "across" the boundary between right and wrong (Latin prefix *trans-* = "across," "change"). An *egress* is an exit (Latin prefix *e-*, *ex-* = "out"; a "stepping out" from an area).

Important social studies words that are built on this base include *gradual, aggressor, congress, progressive,* and *transgress*.

For a glossary of words with this root, see the Digital Resource CD (filename: rootsglossary.pdf).

Name: _____ Date: _____

About the Root: Civics:
Congress

· ·

Directions: Read the information. Then answer the questions.

The Latin base *grad-, gress-* means "step," "go." This base appears in many words you may know, but you may not have thought about their base meaning of "step," "go."

In some *grad-, gress-* words, the idea of "stepping," "going" is literal, referring to physical stepping. As mercury rises in a *centigrade* thermometer, for example, it moves up one "step" at a time over 100 degrees.

But in most *grad-, gress-* words, the "stepping," "going" is figurative. When a teacher *digresses* from the topic, he or she may "step" apart from the subject (while physically staying still). When we *graduate* from high school, we take a "step" ahead in our educational lives.

Think about the meaning of the phrases below. Discuss with a partner how they mean "step" or "go."

◎ working *gradually*

◎ making *progress* on a big assignment

In the United States, *Congress* is the bicameral legislative body of the federal government. The word *bicameral* means "having two chambers." These two chambers are intended to "step together" as they make laws. This is why we call them the *Congress*. The two chambers are the House of Representatives and the Senate. Members of Congress, including Senators and Representatives, have two major jobs. One is to represent the local interests of the people who have elected them. The other is to make laws that will serve the nation as a whole. Sometimes, these two responsibilities conflict. Perhaps this is one of the reasons why legislative change is so *gradual* in the United States. We make *progress* one "step" at a time.

◎ Give an example of a law passed by the House and Senate that affected the nation as a whole. Do you believe it was a good or a poor law? Explain why on a separate sheet of paper.

◎ Now give an example of how representing local interests might conflict with national interests on a separate sheet of paper.

Name: _____ Date: _____

About the Root: Economics:
Progressive and Regressive Taxes

Directions: Read the information. Then answer the question.

Taxes are the primary source of income for governments at all levels. Of the many types of taxes, *progressive* and *regressive* taxes show differences in tax philosophy.

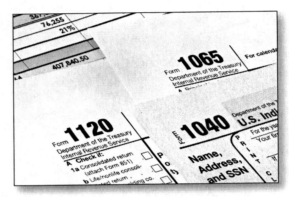

Progressive tax rates vary. Income tax is *progressive* because the tax rate depends on income. The more a person makes, the higher his or her taxes are. *Regressive* taxes, by contrast, do not vary. They are always the same, because they are based on the value of the goods purchased, not on the income of the buyer.

Both kinds of taxes have supporters and detractors. Those who like *progressive* taxes argue that people who make more money can afford to pay higher taxes. Those who dislike *progressive* taxes believe they violate the principle of equality under the law.

◎ If you were a taxpayer, would you prefer *progressive* or *regressive* taxes? Explain your thinking.

_____

_____

_____

_____

_____

_____

_____

Name: _____ Date: _____

About the Root: Politics:
The Diversity of Political Views

Directions: Read the information. Then answer the question.

In a democratic society, people hold a wide range of political opinions. The words we use to describe ourselves say a lot about the way we look at the world.

Conservatives, for example, maintain the status quo. They want to "save," "keep" things "together" as they currently are. They place a high value on time-honored traditions.

Liberals, by contrast, want to "free" themselves from old-fashioned ways and traditions.

Progressives value *progress* and moving "ahead" one "step" at a time. They believe that government should lead the country in making forward-looking changes and reforms.

This may all sound quite modern, but in ancient Rome, a comedian named Terence said, "Quot homines tot sententiae." This is Latin for "There are as many opinions as there are people."

◎ What are *your* political views? Are you a conservative, a liberal, or a progressive? Explain your thinking.

_____

_____

_____

_____

Name: _____ Date: _____

Divide and Conquer:
Gradual Progress

Directions: Use the Base/Prefix Bank to help you identify the roots of the words below. *X* means the word does not contain that element. Write the letter from the Definition Bank for the correct word.

Base/Prefix Bank

ad-/ag- = "to," "toward," "add to"

con- = "with," "together"

pro- = "forward," "ahead"

trans- = "across," "change"

Definition Bank

A. incremental; proceeding by small degrees

B. a violation of a law or moral prohibition

C. advocating change and reform

D. body of legislators assigned to work together to create laws

E. one who commits an unprovoked attack

Word	First Base/ Prefix Means	Second Base/ Suffix Means	Definition
1. aggressor			
2. transgression			
3. progressive			
4. congress			
5. gradual		X	

Name: _____ Date: _____

Making Connections:
Who/What Am I?

· ·

Directions: Match each phrase in the first column with its speaker in the second column.

Phrase	Speaker
_____ **1.** a progressive	**A.** I make laws in the House of Representatives.
_____ **2.** an aggressor	**B.** I am a sinner.
_____ **3.** a congressman	**C.** I believe we should go back to the old way of doing things.
_____ **4.** an egress	**D.** I attack other countries before they have done anything to me.
_____ **5.** a regressive	**E.** I am an exit.
_____ **6.** a transgressor	**F.** I am an extended side-comment, wandering far away from the topic.
_____ **7.** a digression	**G.** I believe in social change and progress.

You Try It!

Use two of the words *gradual, digress,* or *aggressive* in your own sentences:

_____

_____

_____

_____

_____

_____

Base *cid-, cis-*

cid-, cis- = "cut," "kill"

Standards

Uses common, grade-appropriate Greek or Latin affixes and roots as clues to the meaning of a word

Determines the meaning of words and phrases as they are used in a text, including vocabulary specific to domains related to history/social studies

By the end of the year, reads and comprehends literary nonfiction in the grades 6–8 text complexity band proficiently, with scaffolding as needed at the high end of the range

Materials

- *About the Root: Cut That Out* (page 173)

- *About the Root: World History: Genocide* (page 174)

- *About the Root: United States History: John Wilkes Booth, Self-Proclaimed "Tyrannicide!"* (page 175)

- *Divide and Conquer: Cutting and Killing* (page 176)

- *Making Connections: Complete the Sentence* (page 177)

Teacher Preparation

- Read and review the background information about the base *cid-, cis-* on page 172 to familiarize yourself with its context in social studies and government.

- Read and review the glossary of the base found on the Digital Resource CD (filename: rootsglossary.pdf) for additional support.

Guided Practice

About the Root

1. Distribute copies of pages 173, 174, and/or 175 to students. Write *cid-* and *cis-* on the board and discuss their meanings ("cut," "kill"). Ask partners to think about words they already know with this base. Invite sharing.

2. Have students read the passages and answer the questions. Students can work independently or with partners. You may want to conclude with a whole-class discussion to review students' answers and reinforce the meaning of the roots in context.

Divide and Conquer

3. Distribute copies of *Divide and Conquer* (page 176). As you guide students through the activity page, use questions like these to generate discussion about each of the words.

   - Where is the meaning of "cut" or "kill" in the word _____?

   - Where might you see the word _____?

   - Can you think of an example of _____?

Base *cid-*, *cis-* (cont.)

Making Connections

4. Distribute copies of *Making Connections* (page 177).

5. Have students read all of the sentences before completing the activity sheet.

6. Conclude with a whole-class discussion that focuses on root meaning. You may also ask partners to rewrite sentences maintaining meaning but not using the *cid-*, *cis-* words.

Words with *cid-*, *cis-*

concise
concision
decide
decision
decisive
excise
fratricide
herbicide
homicide
incision
incisive
infanticide
insecticide
matricide
patricide
precise
precision
regicide
sororicide
suicide
tyrannicide
uxoricide

A list of words to print out for students can be found on the Digital Resource CD (filename: wordlists.pdf).

Teacher Background Information and Tips

Base *cid -, cis-* = "cut," "kill"

The Latin base *cid-, cis-,* meaning "cut," "kill," appears in social studies words describing cutting and killing. In some words, the idea of "cutting" or "killing" is literal. For example, an *incision* is a "cut" made "into" a surface or body with a sharp knife. A person who commits *suicide* "kills" himself or herself. An *insecticide* "kills" insects. The meaning "kill" is a derivative of the meaning "cut," referring to the knife or sword as the original killing instrument before the invention of gunpowder.

In other *cid-, cis-* words, the idea of "cutting" is figurative. *Incisive* comments are penetrating, as if "cutting" "to" the heart of an issue. A *concise* statement is short and terse, as if "very" "cut" or trimmed (Latin prefix *con-* = "with," "together"; "very"). The figurative "sharpness" of the word *concise* (meaning "brief," "terse," expressed in few words") is suggested by the related phrase, "*cut* to the point," or when a speaker is *concise* and "*cuts* it short." When we *decide* or make a *decision*, we figuratively "cut" "off" our options (Latin prefix *de-* = "down," "off," suggesting the downward fall of a knife or cleaver as it chops). The metaphor of "cutting" underlies the phrase "cut-off date" for rendering a final *decision.* The words *precise* and *precision* are also from this base, referring to "cutting" something "before" it becomes larger (Latin prefix *pre-* = "before"). Thus, *precise* means "exact," "cut to the perfect size."

Many "killing" words from history end in -*cide.* In such words, the first base (almost always followed by a connecting *i*) indicates the target or victim of the killing. Many such words refer both to the act of killing and to the person who commits the deed.

Important social studies words that are built on this base include *patricide, regicide, concise,* and *genocide.*

For a glossary of words with this root, see the Digital Resource CD (filename: rootsglossary.pdf).

Name: _____ Date: _____

About the Root:
Cut That Out

Directions: Read the information. Then answer the questions.

The Latin base *cid-, cis-* means "cut," "kill." In some words, the idea of "cutting" or "killing" is literal. You may already know such words as *homicide*, *insecticide*, or *suicide*, all of which describe actual "killing." When a surgeon makes an *incision*, an actual "cut" is made "into" the body. In the process, a tumor may be *excised*, literally "cut out."

Many other *cid-, cis-* words, however, express the idea of "cutting" in a figurative sense, as in the words *incisive* and *decide*. *Incisive* comments "cut" "into" the heart of an issue without using a knife. When we *decide,* we "cut" "off" other options.

Explain how these words and phrases include the idea of "cutting" or "killing."

◎ The politician's comments were *incisive*.

_____

_____

_____

◎ He had committed the atrocious crime of *patricide.*

_____

_____

_____

Name: _____ Date: _____

About the Root: World History:
Genocide

· ·

Directions: Read the information. Then answer the questions.

Genocide is the planned destruction of a group of people. These may be ethnic, racial, national, or religious groups. Social scientists have studied these horrific acts and identified processes often used in *genocides*. First, an "us vs. them" attitude is created. Next, the targeted group of people is dehumanized. They are characterized as symbols of evil. Finally, the group is exterminated.

Unfortunately, world history provides many examples of genocide. Toward the end of World War I, members of the Ottoman Empire in Turkey killed many Armenians, Assyrians, and Greeks. This came to be called *genocide*. More than six million European Jews died during the Holocaust. This was state-sponsored murder in Nazi Germany during World War II. It was after this horrific event that the United Nations officially defined *genocide*. More recently, many have described battles in the Darfur region of the Sudan in Africa as *genocide*.

◎ Why do you think *genocides* occur?

_____

_____

_____

_____

◎ The word *genocide* is built on the same base as the word *homicide*. How is *genocide* similar to *homicide*? In what important way are they different?

_____

_____

_____

Name: _____ Date: _____

About the Root: United States History:

John Wilkes Booth, Self-Proclaimed "Tyrannicide!"

Directions: Read the information. Then answer the questions.

On April 14, 1865, the actor John Wilkes Booth assassinated President Abraham Lincoln in Ford's Theatre, Washington, DC. He aimed a pistol at the president's head and cried, "*Sic semper tyrannis!*" This Latin phrase means "Thus always to tyrants!"

Booth apparently thought he was performing *tyrannicide*, "the killing of a tyrant." In calling Lincoln a tyrant, Booth ignored his murderous act and presented himself as a Latin-speaking hero. The event occurred in a theater. Booth was play-acting even as he shot, uttering classical lines for the audience to hear.

Legend has it that, when Marcus Junius Brutus stabbed Julius Caesar to death in Rome on the Ides of March in 44 B.C., the murderer cried out the same phrase, "*Sic semper tyrannis!*" Brutus thought he was saving Rome from the dictator Caesar.

In his delusion, Booth saw himself as saving the United States from a tyrannical president. Both men spoke the same lines. But no boast can conceal the horror of murder. As the ancient Greek Euripides (yoo-RIP-i-deez) wrote, "It is one thing to commit an injustice. But to dress up the foul deed with fine words makes the horror even worse!"

◎ Write your opinion about Euripides's comment. Do you agree or disagree with it? Why?

_____

_____

_____

_____

◎ The word *tyrannicide* is built on the same base as the word *regicide* (*reg-* means "king"). How is *tyrannicide* similar to *regicide*? In what way are they different?

_____

_____

_____

_____

Name: _____   Date: _____

Divide and Conquer:
Cutting and Killing

Directions: Use the Base/Prefix Bank to help you identify the roots of the words below. Write the letter from the Definition Bank for the correct word.

Base/Prefix Bank

con- = "with," "together," "very"   *gen(o)-* = "race"   *reg(i)-* = "king"
hom(i)- = "man," "human being"   *in-* = "in," "on," "into"

Definition Bank

A. the assassination of a king

B. a cut made into an object with a sharp knife

C. expressed in few words

D. the killing of a human being

E. the destruction of an entire race of people

Word	First Base/ Prefix Means	Second Base/ Suffix Means	Definition
1. genocide			
2. regicide			
3. concise			
4. incision			
5. homicide			

Name: _____ Date: _____

Making Connections:
Complete the Sentence

Directions: Use the words in the Word Bank to complete the sentences.

Word Bank

| fratricide | homicidal | incisive | patricide | pesticides |

Sentences

1. In Greek mythology, Oedipus Rex committed _____. He killed a stranger at a crossroads, not realizing that the traveler was his own father.

2. The speaker made several _____ comments that cut straight to the heart of the issue.

3. Jack the Ripper was a serial killer whom history will always remember as a _____ maniac.

4. _____ was not uncommon during the American Civil War, in which brothers from northern and southern states found themselves on opposite sides.

5. You should thoroughly wash fruits and vegetables before eating in order to remove the dangerous _____ which have been sprayed on them.

You Try It!

Use two of the following words in your own sentences: *concise, incision,* or *decisive.* Leave blanks for the words. Then ask a classmate to fill in the blanks.

_____

_____

_____

_____

_____

Answer Key

Unit I: Lesson 1–Base *arch-*, *-archy*

About the Root: Chiefs and Leaders (page 22)

one; all men; answers will vary

About the Root: Who is the First Builder? (page 23)

Answers will vary.

About the Root: World History: Archduke Ferdinand and Queen Victoria (page 24)

Answers will vary.

Divide and Conquer: Who Is the Ruler? (page 25)

1. C
2. B
3. E
4. D
5. A

Making Connections: Who Am I? (page 26)

1. D
2. G
3. H
4. F
5. A
6. B
7. C
8. E
9. I

You Try It! Answers will vary.

Unit I: Lesson 2–Suffix *crat-*, *-cracy*

About the Root Activities (page 30–32)

Answers will vary.

About the Root: Government: What Is an Autocracy? (page 31)

Answers will vary.

About the Root: Government: What Is a Bureaucracy? (page 32)

Answers will vary.

Divide and Conquer: Who Is the Ruler? (page 33)

1. B
2. A
3. D
4. C
5. E

Making Connections: Who/What Am I? (page 34)

1. D
2. E
3. F
4. G
5. A
6. B
7. C

You Try It! Answers will vary.

Unit I: Lesson 3–Base *dic-*, *dict-*

About the Root: World History: What is a Dictator? (page 38)

Answers will vary.

About the Root: Government: *Dict-* in the Law (page 39)

Answers will vary.

About the Root: World History: What Was the Edict of Milan? (page 40)

Answers will vary.

Divide and Conquer: Saying, Speaking, Telling (page 41)

1. C
2. B
3. A
4. D
5. E

Making Connections: Who/What Am I? (page 42)

A = 9	B = 2	C = 7
D = 4	E = 6	F = 8
G = 5	H = 10	I = 3

Magic Number: 18.

Answer Key *(cont.)*

Unit I: Lesson 4–Base *judg-, judic-*

About the Root: Government: The Supreme Court (page 46)

the judge, answers will vary

About the Root: Culture and Society: Prejudice (pages 47)

Answers will vary.

About the Root: Government: Sub Judice (page 48)

Answers will vary.

Divide and Conquer: You Be the Judge (page 49)

1. D	**3.** C	**5.** A
2. B	**4.** E	

Making Connections: Complete the Sentence (page 50)

1. injudicious	**3.** prejudice	**5.** judicial
2. misjudged	**4.** adjudicated	

You Try It! Answers will vary.

Unit I: Lesson 5–Bases *popul-* and *dem(o)-*

About the Root Activities (page 54–56)

Answers will vary.

Divide and Conquer: Of, By, and For the People (page 57)

1. E	**2.** B	**3.** C	**4.** A	**5.** D

Making Connections: Riddles (page 58)

Riddle #1: *democracy*

Riddle #2: *epidemic*

Riddle #3: *populist*

You Try It! Answers will vary.

Unit II: Lesson 1–Bases *urb-, urban-* and *poli-, -polis*

About the Root Activities (page 62–64)

Answers will vary.

Divide and Conquer: City Living (page 65)

1. D	**3.** B	**5.** E
2. A	**4.** C	

Making Connections: Who/What Am I? (page 66)

1. B	**3.** D	**5.** A
2. E	**4.** F	**6.** C

You Try It! Answers will vary.

Unit II: Lesson 2–Bases *civ-, cit-, civil-* and *milit-*

About the Root Activities (page 70–72)

Answers will vary.

Divide and Conquer: Soldiers and Citizens (page 73)

1. C	**3.** D	**5.** E
2. B	**4.** A	

Answer Key (cont.)

Making Connections: Word Sort (page 74)

Could describe a person	Could not describe a person
civil	incivility
civil behavior	civil strife
uncivil	civility
civilized	civil rights
uncivilized	
Positive word/phrase	**Negative word/ phrase**
civil	civil strife
civil behavior	incivility
civility	uncivil
civil rights	uncivilized
civilized	
Person or idea	**Describing word**
civil strife	civil
civil behavior	incivility
civil rights	civility
	uncivil
	civilized
	uncivilized

Unit II: Lesson 3—Base *sequ-*, *secut-*

About the Root Activities (page 78–80)
Answers will vary.

Divide and Conquer: Follow the Leader (page 81)

1. E   2. D   3. B   4. A   5. C

Making Connections: Making Meaning (page 82)
Answers will vary.

Unit II: Lesson 4—Base *equ(i)-*, *egal-*

About the Root Activities (page 86–87)
Answers will vary.

Divide and Conquer: Fairness and Equality (page 88)

1. B   2. C   3. D   4. A   5. E

Making Connections: Complete the Sentence (page 89)

1. equator   3. equivocated   5. inadequate
2. egalitarian   4. inequity   6. equitable

You Try It! Answers will vary.

Answer Key (cont.)

Unit II: Lesson 5–Bases *greg-* and *integr-*

About the Root Activities (page 93–95)
Answers will vary.

Divide and Conquer: Together and Apart (page 96)

1. D   2. A   3. E   4. B   5. C

Making Connections: Who/What Am I? (page 97)

1. B   3. F   5. A   7. G
2. C   4. E   6. D

You Try It! Answers will vary.

Unit III: Lesson 1–Bases *the(o)-* and *de(i)-, divin-*

About the Root Activities (page 101–103)
Answers will vary.

Divide and Conquer: One or Many? (page 104)

1. E   2. A   3. C   4. B   5. D

Making Connections: Who/What Are We? (page 105)

1. B   3. C   5. E   7. G
2. D   4. A   6. F

You Try It! Answers will vary.

Unit III: Lesson 2–Base *vert-, vers-*

About the Root Activities (pages 109–111)
Answers will vary.

Divide and Conquer: Many Changes (page 112)

1. B   2. E   3. A   4. D   5. C

Making Connections: Fill in the Blank (page 113)

1. convert   3. avert   5. controversial
2. subversives   4. version

You Try It! Answers will vary.

Unit III: Lesson 3–Bases *human-* and *anthrop(o)-*

About the Root Activities (pages 117–119)
Answers will vary.

Divide and Conquer: Being Human (page 120)

1. B   2. A   3. E   4. D   5. C

Making Connections: Who/What Am I? (page 121)

1. C   3. E   5. F   7. D
2. G   4. A   6. B   8. H

You Try It! Answers will vary.

Answer Key (cont.)

Unit III: Lesson 4–Bases serv-, servat- and liber-, liberat-

About the Root Activities (pages 125–127)
Answers will vary.

Divide and Conquer: To Keep, To Set Free (page 128)

1. D   2. A   3. E   4. C   5. B

Making Connections: Role Playing (page 129)
Answers will vary.

Unit III: Lesson 5–Bases fid-, fidel- and cred-, credit-

About the Root Activities (pages 133–135)
Answers will vary.

Divide and Conquer: Believe It or Not! (page 136)

1. B   2. D   3. E   4. A   5. C

Making Connections: Crossword Puzzle (page 137)

Across	Down
1. confidence	1. confidant
5. credible	2. creditor
6. confident	3. Fido
7. incredible	4. fidelity

Unit IV: Lesson 1–Bases bell- and pac-

About the Root Activities (pages 141–143)
Answers will vary.

Divide and Conquer: Make Peace, Not War (page 144)

1. D   2. E   3. A   4. C   5. B

Making Connections: Who/What Are We? (page 145)

1. F   3. D   5. E   7. G
2. C   4. A   6. B

You Try It! Answers will vary.

Unit IV: Lesson 2–Base annu-, enni-

About the Root: Year After Year (page 149)
Answers will vary.

About the Root: Culture and Society: Can You Count in Latin? (page 150)
200 years; 150 years; 300 years

About the Root: United States History: The Bicentennial (page 151)
Answers will vary.

Answer Key (cont.)

Divide and Conquer: How Many Years? (page 152)

1. A   2. E   3. B   4. D   5. C

Making Connections: What Am I? (page 153)

1. H   3. E   5. G   7. A

2. C   4. B   6. F   8. D

You Try It! Answers will vary.

Unit IV: Lesson 3–Base *stru-, struct-*

About the Root: Activities (pages 157–159)

Answers will vary.

Divide and Conquer: Taking Apart Building Words (page 160)

1. A   2. E   3. D   4. B   5. C

Making Connections: Let's Build Words (page 161)

Answers will vary.

Unit IV: Lesson 4–Base *grad-, gress-*

About the Root Activities (pages 165–167)

Answers will vary.

Divide and Conquer: Gradual Progress (page 168)

1. E   2. B   3. C   4. D   5. A

Making Connections: Who/What Am I? (page 169)

1. G   3. A   5. C   7. F

2. D   4. E   6. B

Unit IV: Lesson 5–Base *grad-, gress-*

About the Root Activities (pages 173–175)

Answers will vary.

Divide and Conquer: Cutting and Killing (page 176)

1. E   2. A   3. C   4. B   5. D

Making Connections: Complete the Sentence (page 177)

1. patricide

2. incisive

3. homicidal

4. fraticide

5. pesticides

References Cited

ACT, Inc. *Reading Between the Lines: What the ACT Reveals About College Readiness in Reading.* Iowa City, IA: Author, 2006.

Baumann, James, Elizabeth C. Carr-Edwards, George Font, Cathleen A. Tereshinski, Edward J. Kame'enui, and Stephen Olejnik. "Teaching Morphemic and Contextual Analysis to Fifth-Grade Students." *Reading Research Quarterly* 37 (2002): 150–176.

Baumann, James F., George Font, Elizabeth C. Edwards, and Eileen Boland. "Strategies for Teaching Middle-Grade Students to Use Word-Part and Context Clues to Expand Reading Vocabulary." In *Teaching and Learning Vocabulary: Bringing Research to Practice*, edited by Elfrieda H. Hiebert and Michael L. Kamil, 179–205. Mahwah, NJ: Erlbaum, 2005.

Bear, Donald, Marcia Invernizzi, Shane Templeton, and Francine R. Johnston. *Words Their Way (5th Edition).* Upper Saddle River, NJ: Prentice Hall, 2011.

Beck, Isabel L., Margaret G. McKeown, and Linda Kucan. *Bringing Words to Life: Robust Vocabulary Instruction.* New York: Guilford, 2002.

Beck, Isabel, Charles A. Perfetti, and Margaret G. McKeown. "Effects of Long-Term Vocabulary Instruction on Lexical Access and Reading Comprehension." *Journal of Educational Psychology* 74 (1982): 506–521.

Biemiller, Andrew. "Implications for Choosing Words for Primary Grade Vocabulary." In *Teaching and Learning Vocabulary: Bringing Research to Practice*, edited by by Elfrieda H. Hiebert and Michael L. Kamil, 223–242. Mahwah, NJ: Erlbaum, 2005.

Biemiller, Andrew, and Naomi Slonim. "Estimating Root Word Vocabulary Growth in Normative and Advantaged Populations: Evidence for a Common Sequence of Vocabulary Acquisition." *Journal of Educational Psychology* 93 (2001): 498–520.

Blachowicz, Camille, and Peter Fisher. *Teaching Vocabulary in All Classrooms (3rd Edition).* Upper Saddle River, NJ: Pearson/Merrill/Prentice Hall, 2006.

Blachowicz, Camille, Peter Fisher, Donna Ogle, and Susan Watts-Taffe. "Vocabulary: Questions from the Classroom." *Reading Research Quarterly* 41 (2006): 524–538.

Carlisle, Joanne F. "Awareness of the Structure and Meaning of Morphologically Complex Words: Impact on Reading." *Reading and Writing: An Interdisciplinary Journal* 12 (2000): 169–190.

———. "Effects of Instruction in Morphological Awareness on Literacy Achievement: An Integrative Review." *Reading Research Quarterly* 45 (2010): 464–487.

Chandler, Richard E., and Kessel Schwartz. *A New History of Spanish Literature.* Baton Rouge, LA: LSU Press, 1961/1991.

Cunningham, Patricia M. *Phonics They Use: Words for Reading and Writing.* New York: Longman, 2004.

References Cited (cont.)

Eusebius. *The History of the Church*. New York: Penguin, 322.1989.

Graves, M.F., and S.M. Watts-Taffe. "The Place of Word Consciousness in a Research-Based Vocabulary Program." In *What Research Has to Say About Reading Instruction*, edited by Alan E. Farstrup and S. Jay Samuels, 140–165. Newark, DE: International Reading Association, 2002.

Harmon, Janis M., Wanda B. Hedrick, and Karen D. Wood. "Research on Vocabulary Instruction in the Content Areas: Implications for Struggling Readers." *Reading & Writing Quarterly* 21 (2005): 261–280.

Kame'enui, Edward J., Douglas W. Carnine, and Roger Freschi. "Effects of Text Construction and Instructional Procedures for Teaching Word Meanings on Comprehension and Recall." *Reading Research Quarterly* 17 (1982): 367–388.

Kieffer, Michael, and Nonie K. Lesaux. "Breaking Down Words to Build Meaning: Morphology, Vocabulary, and Reading Comprehension in the Urban Classroom." *The Reading Teacher* 61 (2007): 134–144.

LaFleur, Richard A. "Latin Students Score High On SAT and Achievement Tests." Classical Journal, 76 (3), 254. 1981.

Lehr, Fran, Jean Osborn, and Elfrieda H. Hiebert. "Research-Based Practices in Early Reading Series: A Focus on Vocabulary." 2004. http://www.eric.ed.gov/?id=ED483190.

Mountain, Lee. "ROOTing Out Meaning: More Morphemic Analysis for Primary Pupils." *The Reading Teacher* 58 (2005): 742–749.

Nagy, William, Richard C. Anderson, Marlene Schommer, Judith Ann Scott, and Anne C. Stallman. "Morphological Families in the Internal Lexicon." *Reading Research Quarterly* 24 (1989): 262–282.

Nagy, William, and Judith Ann Scott. "Vocabulary Processes." In *Handbook of Reading Research*, Vol. III, edited by Michael L. Kamil, Peter B. Mosenthal, P. David Pearson, and Rebecca Barr, 269–284. Mahwah, NJ: Erlbaum, 2000.

Porter-Collier, I.M. "Teaching Vocabulary Through the Roots Approach in order to Increase Comprehension and Metacognition." Unpublished masters degree project. Akron OH: University of Akron, 2010.

Rasinski, Timothy, and Nancy Padak. *From Phonics to Fluency (3rd Edition)*. New York: Longman, 2013.

Rasinski, Timothy, Nancy Padak, Evangeline Newton, and Rick M. Newton. *Greek and Latin Roots: Keys to Building Vocabulary*. Huntington Beach, CA: Shell Educational Publishing, 2008.

Stahl, Steven A., and Marilyn M. Fairbanks. "The Effects of Vocabulary Instruction: A Model-Based Meta-Analysis." *Review of Educational Research* 56 (1986): 72–110.

Additional Practice Activities

Use the following activities to provide extra practice, to share with parents, or to differentiate instruction.

Be the Bard

Although most people recognize William Shakespeare as a great writer of plays and poetry, few realize that he was a great wordsmith. It has been estimated that Shakespeare invented approximately eight percent or one of every twelve unique words that he used. Many of these words were simply compounds made of already existing base words and/ or affixes. Words such as *lackluster*, *premeditated*, and *noiseless* are but a few examples of the words he created. We think Shakespeare is a pretty good fellow to emulate. In *Be the Bard*, students create new words by using already learned roots. Student-invented words are put on display, and the inventor is asked to explain the meaning of his or her creation. Here are some words students invented: *automand* (an order that one gives to himself or herself), *terrameter* (a device for measuring land), and *contraduct* (to lead a group against another group). Although these created words are fanciful, students take genuine delight in using meaningful roots and affixes to create even more meaning.

Concentration (or Memory)

Select eight to ten words containing a root/base. Make double sets of word cards for each (or put the word and its definition on separate cards). Shuffle the cards and place them all facedown on a table. Players take turns trying to make matches. The player with the most matches wins the game.

Go Fish

Select four to six bases. For each, create a set of four words. Students use these to play "Go Fish."

Word War

Provide words containing the targeted base (or bases) written on cards. Play the card game "war" with them. Each player turns up a card. The person whose card a) comes first in alphabetical order, b) has more letters, or c) has more syllables wins the round, as long as he or she can say both words and their meanings. If the words are similar, players draw again, and the same rules apply. The player who wins this "war" takes all the cards. A player who gets all his or her partner's cards wins the game.

Additional Practice Activities *(cont.)*

List-Group-Label or Word Webs

Provide a base. Ask students to brainstorm words containing it. Write these on the board or chart paper. Then ask small groups to work with the words by:

◎ listing related terms and providing labels for them.

◎ developing a graphic, such as a web, that shows how the words are related.

◎ writing a summary text, using the grouping of words as an outline.

Root Word Riddles

Who doesn't enjoy solving a riddle? This strategy invites students to create and guess riddles with words from the same base. Give pairs of students a list of words that contain the targeted base. Each pair's job is to devise riddles for other students to solve. (You may want to model riddle creation for students.) See an example for *invisible* on the right.

Sketch to Stretch

Provide words written on slips of paper and distribute to students. Ask them to sketch something that reveals the word meaning. Then they share these with others to guess.

> **invisible**
>
> 1. I have four syllables.
>
> 2. I have two word parts.
>
> 3. One part means "not."
>
> 4. The other means "see."
>
> 5. I mean not perceptible by the human eye.
>
> What am I?

Twenty Questions

Students take turns asking questions that will help them figure out a "mystery" word that contains the targeted base. (If you and students keep a word wall of words containing the base, select words from it. Otherwise, you can list several words on the chalkboard.) They can ask up to 20 yes or no questions to try to determine the word.

Word Skits

List eight to ten words containing the targeted base on the board. Divide students into teams of three or four. Each team chooses one word and writes its definition on an index card. Working together, they create a skit that shows the meaning of the word. The skit is performed without words. Classmates try to guess the word being shown. Once the word is correctly identified, the definition is read out loud.

Additional Practice Activities (cont.)

Wordo

List twenty-four words containing the targeted base on the board. Duplicate a 4 x 4 or 5 x 5 Wordo Matrix for each student found on the Digital Resource CD (filenames: 4x4wordomatrix.pdf, 5x5wordomatrix.pdf). Ask students to choose a free box and mark it. Then have them write one of the words in each of the remaining boxes. Call a clue for each word: the definition, a synonym, an antonym, or a sentence with the target word deleted. Students figure out the correct target word, then put an *X* through it. (If you want to clear the sheets and play again, use small scraps of paper or other items to mark the squares.) When a student has *X*'s or markers in a row, column, diagonal, or four corners he or she can call out "Wordo!"

Word puzzles

Make crossword puzzles or word searches using http://www.puzzlemaker.com.

Word Sorts

Select about ten words containing the targeted root. Put the words on index cards. Provide one set of word cards to each pair of students. Ask students to group the words. Remind them that they will have to explain their groupings. Grouping may include:

◎ presence/absence of a prefix or suffix

◎ number of syllables

◎ presence/absence of a long vowel sound (in general, or a particular long vowel sound)

◎ words that refer to liquids and words that don't

◎ words that "cut" and words that don't

Invite students to tell about one of their groups, both the words contained in it and the reason for putting them together. Ask students to sort the same set of words in a different way. Each sort provides students another opportunity to think about both the words and their component parts.

Word Spokes

Duplicate a Word Spokes template for each student or pair of students found on the Digital Resource CD (filename: wordspokeschart.pdf). Put the targeted base or prefix on the board. Ask students to identify enough words containing the base to complete the chart. You may want to ask students to add sentences or illustrations of selected words, as well. Conclude the activity with sharing.

Contents of the Digital Resource CD

	Student Resources	
Page	**Title**	**Filename**
22–26	Unit I Lesson 1—Base *arch-, -archy*	arch_archy.pdf
30–34	Unit I Lesson 2—Base *-crat, -cracy*	crat_cracy.pdf
38–42	Unit I Lesson 3—Base *dic-, dict-*	dic_dict.pdf
46–50	Unit I Lesson 4—Base *judg-, judic-*	judg_judic.pdf
54–58	Unit I Lesson 5—Bases *popul-* and *dem(o)-*	popul_dem.pdf
62–66	Unit II Lesson 1—Bases *urb-, urban-* and *poli-, -polis*	urb_urban_poli_polis.pdf
70–74	Unit II Lesson 2—Bases *civ-, cit-, civil-* and *milit-*	civ_cit_civil_milit.pdf
78–82	Unit II Lesson 3—Base *sequ-, secut-*	sequ_secut.pdf
86–89	Unit II Lesson 4—Base *equ(i)-, egal-*	equ_egal.pdf
93–97	Unit II Lesson 5—Bases *greg-* and *integr-*	greg_integr.pdf
101–105	Unit III Lesson 1—Bases *the(o)-* and *de(i)-, divin-*	the_de_divin.pdf
109–113	Unit III Lesson 2—Base *vert-, vers-*	vert_vers.pdf
117–121	Unit III Lesson 3—Bases *human-* and *anthrop(o)-*	human_anthropo.pdf
125–129	Unit III Lesson 4—Bases *serv-, servat-* and *liber-, liberat-*	serv_servat_liber_liberat.pdf
133–137	Unit III Lesson 5—Bases *fid-, fidel-* and *cred-, credit-*	fid_fidel_cred_credit.pdf
141–145	Unit IV Lesson 1—Bases *bell-* and *pac-*	bell_pac.pdf
149–153	Unit IV Lesson 2—Base *annu-, enni-*	annu_enni.pdf
157–161	Unit IV Lesson 3—Base *stru-, struct-*	stru_struct.pdf
165–169	Unit IV Lesson 4—Base *grad-, gress-*	grad_gress.pdf
173–177	Unit IV Lesson 5—Base *cid-, cis-*	cid_cis.pdf

	Teacher Resources	
Pages	**Resource**	**Filename**
16	Standards Chart	standards.pdf
NA	Functions of Prefixes and Suffixes	functions.pdf
NA	4 x 4 Wordo Matrix	4x4wordomatrix.pdf
NA	5 x 5 Wordo Matrix	5x5wordomatrix.pdf
NA	Word Spokes Chart	wordspokeschart.pdf
NA	Student Word Lists	wordlists.pdf
NA	Flashcards	flashcards.pdf
NA	Roots Glossary	rootsglossary.pdf

Notes

Notes

Notes

#50868—Getting to the Roots of Social Studies Vocabulary